Teenage Behaviors Unraveled: a Comprehensive Guide for Parents and Caregivers

Hagen Laura

Published by Hagen Laura, 2024.

TEENAGE BEHAVIORS UNRAVELED: A COMPREHENSIVE GUIDE FOR PARENTS AND CAREGIVERS

First edition. April 2, 2024.

Copyright © 2024 Hagen Laura.

ISBN: 979-8224219933

Written by Hagen Laura.

Table of Contents

. . . .

- THE DEVELOPMENTAL Stage of Adolescence

Adolescence is a crucial stage in human development that typically occurs between the ages of 10 and 19. During this period, individuals undergo significant physical, cognitive, and emotional changes as they transition from childhood to adulthood. It is a time of exploration, self-discovery, and identity formation, as individuals strive to establish their independence and autonomy while navigating the challenges of adolescence.

One of the hallmark characteristics of adolescence is the onset of puberty, which marks the beginning of physical changes such as growth spurts, development of secondary sexual characteristics, and hormonal fluctuations. These changes can be both exciting and confusing for adolescents, as they grapple with their emerging sexuality and identity. It is important for parents, educators, and other caregivers to provide support and guidance during this time, as adolescents may experience anxiety, self-consciousness, and body image issues as they adjust to their changing bodies.

In addition to physical changes, adolescents also experience significant cognitive development during this stage. They begin to think more abstractly and critically, and their ability to reason, problem-solve, and make decisions improves. This cognitive growth allows adolescents to engage in more complex thinking and to consider multiple perspectives, which is essential for their academic and social development. However, it can also lead to challenges such as risk-taking behavior, impulsivity, and peer pressure, as adolescents navigate the demands of school, relationships, and social expectations.

Emotionally, adolescents may experience a wide range of feelings and emotions as they navigate the sometimes turbulent waters of adolescence. They may struggle with issues of identity, self-esteem, and belonging, as they seek to establish their own sense of self and autonomy. Adolescents may also grapple with mood swings, emotional intensity, and interpersonal conflicts as they learn to navigate the complexities of social relationships and peer dynamics. It is important for caregivers and educators to provide a supportive and understanding environment for adolescents to express their emotions and to develop healthy coping strategies for managing stress and anxiety.

During adolescence, individuals also begin to establish their independence from their parents and caregivers, as they seek to assert their autonomy and make decisions for themselves. This process of individuation can be challenging for both adolescents and their parents, as they navigate the balance between independence and dependence, and as adolescents strive to establish their own identity while maintaining a connection to their families. It is important for parents and caregivers to respect adolescents' need for independence and autonomy, while also providing guidance, support, and boundaries to help them navigate the challenges of adolescence. It is a time of exploration, self-discovery, and identity formation, as adolescents navigate the physical, cognitive, and emotional changes that accompany this stage of development. By providing support, guidance, and understanding, caregivers and educators can help adolescents to navigate the challenges of adolescence and to develop the skills, resilience, and self-awareness needed to thrive in this crucial stage of human development.

- Changes in Brain Development

Brain development is a complex and dynamic process that begins in utero and continues throughout our lives. During this time, the brain undergoes significant changes that shape our cognitive, emotional, and behavioral functioning. One of the key aspects of brain development is neurogenesis, the process by which new neurons are generated. This process is particularly active during early childhood, when the brain is rapidly growing and forming new connections.

As we age, the rate of neurogenesis slows down, but the brain remains highly plastic, meaning it has the ability to adapt and reorganize in response to new experiences and learning. This plasticity is crucial for our ability to learn, remember, and adapt to our environment. However, the extent to which the brain can change is not unlimited, and there are sensitive periods during development when certain skills or abilities are most easily acquired.

One of the most well-known sensitive periods in brain development is the critical period for language acquisition. During this time, typically in early childhood, the brain is highly receptive to learning language. Children who are exposed to multiple languages during this period have been shown to develop the ability to speak and understand them with relative ease. In contrast, individuals who are exposed to new languages later in life may struggle to achieve native-like proficiency.

Another key aspect of brain development is myelination, the process by which neural pathways are insulated with a fatty substance called myelin. This insulation helps to speed up the transmission of electrical signals between neurons, enabling more efficient communication within the brain. Myelination begins in infancy and continues into early adulthood, with different brain regions myelinating at different rates. This process is essential for the development of cognitive functions such as attention, memory, and decision-making.

In addition to neurogenesis and myelination, synaptic pruning is another important process that occurs during brain development. Synaptic pruning involves the elimination of unnecessary or weak connections between neurons, which helps to streamline neural pathways and improve the efficiency of neural communication. This process is particularly active during adolescence, when the brain undergoes significant refinement and specialization.

Changes in brain development can also be influenced by environmental factors such as stress, nutrition, and exposure to toxins. Chronic stress, for example, has been shown to have a negative impact on brain development, particularly in regions associated with memory and emotional regulation. Similarly, malnutrition can impair the growth and functioning of the brain, leading to cognitive deficits and developmental delays.

Understanding the changes that occur in the brain during development is crucial for promoting healthy cognitive, emotional, and social development. By recognizing the sensitive periods in brain development and the factors that can influence neural plasticity, we can provide children and adolescents with the support and opportunities they need to reach their full potential. Through continued research and education, we can further our understanding of brain development and its impact on human behavior and well-being.

- Impact of Hormones

Hormones play a crucial role in the regulation of various bodily functions, from metabolism to mood. These chemical messengers are produced by the endocrine glands and travel throughout the body to target cells, where they elicit specific responses. The impact of hormones on the body is profound and wide-ranging, affecting everything from growth and development to reproduction and stress response.

One of the key functions of hormones is to regulate metabolism. For example, insulin is a hormone produced by the pancreas that helps regulate blood sugar levels. When we eat, our blood sugar levels rise, triggering the release of insulin to help bring them back down to a normal range. Insulin signals the body's cells to take up glucose from the bloodstream and use it for energy or store it for later use. This process is crucial for maintaining stable energy levels and preventing dangerous spikes or dips in blood sugar.

Hormones also play a critical role in growth and development. For example, growth hormone is produced by the pituitary gland and is essential for normal growth in children and adolescents. It stimulates the growth of bones, muscles, and organs, helping children reach their full potential height and size. Without adequate levels of growth hormone, children may experience stunted growth and developmental delays. Similarly, sex hormones such as testosterone and estrogen play a crucial role in the development of secondary sexual characteristics during puberty, shaping physical appearance and reproductive capacity.

In addition to their roles in metabolism and growth, hormones also play a key role in reproductive function. In females, hormones such as estrogen and progesterone regulate the menstrual cycle, ovulation, and pregnancy. Estrogen is responsible for the development of female secondary sexual characteristics, such as breast development and body hair growth. Progesterone helps prepare the uterus for pregnancy and supports fetal development during pregnancy. In males, testosterone is the primary sex hormone responsible for the development of male secondary sexual characteristics, such as facial hair growth and deepening of the voice.

Furthermore, hormones also play a crucial role in the body's stress response. When we encounter a stressful situation, the body releases hormones such as cortisol and adrenaline to help us respond to the threat. These hormones trigger a cascade of physiological changes, such as increased heart rate, rapid breathing, and sharpened focus, that prepare the body to fight or flee from danger. While these stress hormones are essential for survival in acute stress situations, chronic stress can lead to dysregulation of the stress response system, resulting in negative impact on physical and mental health. From metabolism to growth, reproduction, and stress response, hormones influence nearly every aspect of our health and well-being. Understanding the impact of hormones on the body can help us appreciate the complexity of our physiological processes and the importance of maintaining hormonal balance for optimal health. By nurturing our endocrine system through healthy lifestyle choices, such as balanced diet, regular exercise, and stress management, we can support the proper functioning of our hormones and promote overall well-being.

....

- MOOD SWINGS AND EMOTIONAL Fluctuations

Mood swings and emotional fluctuations are common occurrences that affect individuals of all ages and backgrounds. While some people may experience occasional shifts in their mood, others may struggle with more frequent and intense emotional changes. Understanding the underlying causes and potential solutions for mood swings is essential for promoting mental well-being and overall emotional health.

There are various factors that can contribute to mood swings and emotional fluctuations. Biological factors, such as hormonal imbalances, genetic predispositions, and neurological differences, can play a significant role in influencing one's emotional state. For example, fluctuations in estrogen and progesterone levels during the menstrual cycle can lead to mood changes in women. Likewise, imbalances in neurotransmitters, such as serotonin and dopamine, can impact mood regulation and stability.

Psychological factors, such as stress, trauma, and unresolved emotional issues, can also contribute to mood swings. Chronic stress, in particular, can trigger the release of cortisol and adrenaline, leading to heightened emotional reactivity and instability. Traumatic experiences, such as childhood abuse or significant loss, can leave lasting emotional scars that manifest as mood swings and emotional fluctuations in adulthood. Additionally, unresolved conflicts or issues within relationships can cause emotional turmoil and instability.

Moreover, environmental factors, such as lifestyle choices, social interactions, and cultural influences, can impact one's mood and emotional well-being. Poor sleep habits, unhealthy diet, lack of exercise, and substance abuse can all contribute to mood swings and emotional fluctuations. Social isolation, conflicts with loved ones, and negative social comparisons can also undermine emotional stability and contribute to mood swings. Cultural norms and expectations regarding emotional expression and mental health can further shape one's understanding and experience of mood swings.

It is essential to recognize that mood swings and emotional fluctuations are not inherently negative or pathological. It is normal for individuals to experience a range of emotions, from joy and excitement to sadness and anger, in response to different situations and stimuli. However, when these mood changes become excessive, prolonged, or disruptive to one's daily functioning and well-being, they may warrant further attention and intervention.

There are various strategies and techniques that individuals can use to manage and regulate their mood swings and emotional fluctuations. Developing self-awareness and mindfulness practices can help individuals recognize and understand their emotional triggers and responses. By gaining insight into the underlying factors contributing to their mood swings, individuals can cultivate greater emotional resilience and self-control.

Engaging in regular physical activity, maintaining a balanced diet, prioritizing adequate sleep, and managing stress effectively can also help stabilize one's mood and emotions. Healthy lifestyle choices can support overall emotional well-being and reduce the likelihood of experiencing mood swings. Additionally, seeking support from mental health professionals, such as therapists or counselors, can provide individuals with tools and techniques to cope with their mood swings and emotional challenges. By understanding the various factors that contribute to mood swings, such as biological, psychological, and environmental influences, individuals can take proactive steps to manage their emotions effectively. Developing self-awareness, engaging in healthy lifestyle practices, and seeking professional support when needed are essential strategies for promoting emotional stability and resilience. Ultimately, by cultivating greater emotional intelligence and self-care practices, individuals can navigate their mood swings with greater ease and compassion towards themselves.

- Dealing with Stress and Anxiety

Stress and anxiety are common experiences that affect individuals in various aspects of their daily lives. Whether it be due to work pressures, personal relationships, or other external factors, feeling stressed or anxious is a natural response to certain situations. However, prolonged periods of stress and anxiety can have detrimental effects on both physical and mental well-being, making it crucial to address these issues and develop coping strategies to effectively manage them.

One of the first steps in dealing with stress and anxiety is to recognize the signs and symptoms that may be present. This could include feelings of overwhelm, constant worry, irritability, restlessness, or physical symptoms such as headaches, muscle tension, or fatigue. By identifying these indicators, individuals can become more aware of when they are experiencing stress and anxiety and take proactive steps to address them before they escalate.

Once the signs of stress and anxiety have been recognized, it is important to identify the root causes of these feelings. This could involve examining the external triggers that may be contributing to stress, such as excessive workloads, conflict in relationships, financial concerns, or other sources of pressure.

In addition to addressing external stressors, it is also important to focus on internal factors that may be contributing to feelings of anxiety. This could involve examining negative thought patterns, self-criticism, perfectionism, or other cognitive distortions that may be exacerbating feelings of stress. By challenging and reframing these thoughts, individuals can begin to alter their perspective and develop healthier ways of coping with stress and anxiety.

As part of managing stress and anxiety, it is important to prioritize self-care and well-being. This can involve engaging in activities that promote relaxation and reduce stress, such as exercise, meditation, deep breathing, or spending time in nature. Additionally, maintaining a healthy lifestyle through proper nutrition, adequate sleep, and hydration can also play a significant role in managing stress and anxiety.

In some cases, seeking professional help may be beneficial in dealing with stress and anxiety. This could involve speaking with a therapist, counselor, or mental health professional who can provide support, guidance, and strategies for managing stress. Additionally, medication or other treatment options may be recommended for individuals with severe or persistent anxiety symptoms. By recognizing the signs and symptoms of stress, identifying the root causes, challenging negative thought patterns, prioritizing self-care, and seeking professional help when needed, individuals can develop effective coping strategies to manage stress and anxiety in a healthy and sustainable way.

- Peer Pressure and its Influence

Peer pressure is a phenomenon that has been widely recognized and studied in the field of psychology for its significant impact on individuals, especially in adolescence. It refers to the social influence exerted by one's peers, which can lead individuals to conform to group norms or engage in behaviors they may not have chosen otherwise. Peer pressure can manifest in various forms, such as direct persuasion, subtle suggestions, or even non-verbal cues. While peer pressure is often associated with negative outcomes, such as engaging in risky behaviors or substance abuse, it can also have positive effects, such as promoting prosocial behaviors and encouraging personal growth.

One of the key factors that contribute to the influence of peer pressure is the desire for social acceptance and belonging. Adolescents, in particular, are highly sensitive to social cues and seek approval from their peers as they navigate the challenges of identity formation and social development. As a result, they may feel pressured to conform to peer norms in order to maintain their social standing or avoid rejection. This desire for acceptance can override individual values and beliefs, leading individuals to engage in behaviors that they may not necessarily agree with, simply to fit in with their peers.

Another factor that amplifies the influence of peer pressure is the susceptibility to conformity, which is a natural tendency for individuals to adjust their attitudes, beliefs, and behaviors to align with those of a group. This can be attributed to the need for social comparison and the desire to avoid social ostracism. Adolescents, in particular, are at a stage of development where they are more vulnerable to conformity due to their heightened need for peer approval and their still-developing sense of self. As a result, they may be more willing to go along with the crowd, even if it means compromising their own values or making decisions that are not in their best interest.

It is important to note that peer pressure is not inherently negative, as it can also play a constructive role in shaping individuals' behaviors and attitudes. Positive peer pressure can encourage individuals to engage in prosocial behaviors, such as volunteering, helping others, or pursuing academic excellence. In such cases, peers serve as positive role models and sources of motivation, inspiring individuals to strive for personal growth and self-improvement. Additionally, peer support can provide a sense of community and belonging, fostering social connections and promoting emotional well-being.

However, the negative consequences of peer pressure cannot be overlooked, especially when it leads individuals to engage in risky behaviors or make poor decisions. Research has shown that adolescents are particularly susceptible to peer pressure due to their heightened sensitivity to social approval and their desire to establish their identity within peer groups. This vulnerability can make adolescents more likely to conform to peer norms, even if it means engaging in behaviors that are potentially harmful or detrimental to their well-being. In extreme cases, peer pressure can lead to serious consequences, such as substance abuse, delinquency, or involvement in risky sexual behaviors.

To mitigate the negative effects of peer pressure, it is important for individuals to develop strong social skills, assertiveness, and a sense of self-efficacy. By cultivating these qualities, individuals can better resist negative peer influence and make independent and informed decisions based on their own values and beliefs. In addition, fostering positive relationships with peers who share similar values and goals can provide a supportive and encouraging social network that reinforces healthy behaviors and attitudes. By promoting a sense of autonomy and self-confidence, individuals can navigate peer pressure more effectively and resist negative influences that may compromise their well-being. While peer pressure can have both positive and negative effects, it is important for individuals to recognize the impact of peer influence and develop strategies to resist negative pressures and make independent choices. By fostering strong social skills, assertiveness, and self-efficacy, individuals can navigate peer pressure more effectively and make decisions that align with their values and goals. Ultimately, understanding the dynamics of peer pressure and its influence can empower individuals to navigate social interactions more confidently and maintain their individuality in the face of social pressures.

. . . .

- EFFECTIVE LISTENING Skills

Effective listening skills are an essential component of successful communication in both personal and professional settings. Listening is not simply a passive activity where one hears the words being spoken, but rather an active process that requires concentration, empathy, and understanding. By improving our listening skills, we can enhance our relationships, minimize misunderstandings, and foster a more positive and collaborative environment.

One key aspect of effective listening is being fully present in the moment. This means setting aside distractions such as phones, laptops, or other competing stimuli and giving our undivided attention to the speaker. By maintaining eye contact, nodding in acknowledgment, and providing verbal cues such as "I see" or "I understand," we signal to the speaker that we are engaged and receptive to what they are saying. This not only demonstrates respect for the speaker but also encourages them to express themselves more freely and openly.

Another essential component of effective listening is demonstrating empathy and understanding. Empathy involves putting oneself in the shoes of the speaker and trying to see the world from their perspective. This requires active listening, which involves not only hearing the words being spoken but also interpreting their meaning, tone, and underlying emotions. By showing empathy and understanding, we validate the speaker's feelings and experiences, creating a safe space for them to express themselves authentically.

Furthermore, effective listening involves asking clarifying questions and summarizing the speaker's key points. By asking open-ended questions such as "Can you tell me more about that. " or "How did that make you feel. " we encourage the speaker to elaborate on their thoughts and feelings, leading to a deeper and more meaningful conversation. Summarizing the speaker's key points and reflecting them back in our own words helps to ensure that we have understood them correctly and prevents misunderstandings or misinterpretations.

Additionally, effective listening requires being nonjudgmental and nonreactive. It's important to suspend our own judgments, assumptions, or biases and approach the conversation with an open mind. By refraining from interrupting, making premature judgments, or offering unsolicited advice, we create an atmosphere of trust and respect that encourages the speaker to share their thoughts and feelings honestly and openly. This not only fosters better communication but also promotes mutual understanding and empathy. By being fully present in the moment, demonstrating empathy and understanding, asking clarifying questions, summarizing key points, and suspending judgment, we can become better listeners and communicators. Ultimately, improving our listening skills can lead to more productive conversations, deeper connections, and greater mutual respect in both personal and professional relationships.

- Setting Boundaries and Guidelines

Setting boundaries and guidelines is an essential aspect of maintaining healthy relationships and promoting personal well-being. Boundaries can be physical, emotional, or psychological limits that indicate to others how we want to be treated, what behavior is acceptable, and what is unacceptable. Guidelines, on the other hand, are specific rules or standards that help us navigate our interactions with others while respecting both ourselves and the people around us. By establishing clear boundaries and guidelines, we can create a safe and supportive environment where mutual respect and understanding can thrive.

One of the key benefits of setting boundaries and guidelines is that it helps us establish a sense of self-respect and self-worth. When we clearly communicate our needs, values, and limits to others, we are asserting our right to be treated with dignity and respect. By setting boundaries, we are showing that we value ourselves enough to stand up for what we believe in and protect ourselves from harm or mistreatment. This can be empowering and can help boost our self-esteem and self-confidence.

Furthermore, setting boundaries and guidelines can help improve communication and reduce conflicts in relationships. When we clearly define our expectations and limits, we are providing others with valuable information about how they can interact with us in a way that is respectful and considerate. This can prevent misunderstandings, hurt feelings, and resentment that can arise when our boundaries are crossed or our guidelines are ignored. By establishing clear boundaries and guidelines, we are creating a framework for healthy communication and cooperation in our relationships.

In addition, setting boundaries and guidelines can help us protect our emotional and mental well-being. By defining what behavior is acceptable and what is not, we are safeguarding ourselves from toxic relationships, emotional manipulation, and psychological harm. When we establish clear boundaries, we are making a stand against negative influences that can undermine our mental health and emotional stability. By setting guidelines, we are giving ourselves permission to prioritize our own needs and well-being, which is crucial for maintaining a healthy and balanced life.

Another important aspect of setting boundaries and guidelines is that it helps us establish a sense of personal autonomy and agency. When we assert our right to set boundaries and guidelines, we are taking control of our own lives and decisions. This can be empowering and can help us feel more in charge of our own destiny. By setting boundaries and guidelines, we are giving ourselves permission to live according to our own values and beliefs, rather than being dictated by the expectations or demands of others. This can promote a sense of freedom and independence that is essential for personal growth and fulfillment. By establishing clear boundaries and guidelines, we are communicating our needs, values, and limits to others, creating a safe and supportive environment where mutual respect and understanding can thrive. Setting boundaries and guidelines can help improve communication, reduce conflicts, protect our emotional and mental well-being, and promote personal autonomy and agency. Ultimately, setting boundaries and guidelines is a valuable tool for navigating our interactions with others and living a fulfilling and authentic life.

- Building Trust and Connection

Building trust and connection is essential in both personal and professional relationships. Trust is the foundation upon which all relationships are built, and without it, communication and collaboration become difficult. When trust is present, people are more willing to be vulnerable, share their thoughts and feelings, and work together towards common goals. Connection, on the other hand, is the bond that forms between individuals when trust is established. It goes beyond just mere communication and involves truly understanding and empathizing with another person.

One of the key ways to build trust and connection is through effective communication. This involves not only speaking clearly and honestly but also actively listening to others and showing empathy and understanding. When individuals feel like they are being heard and understood, they are more likely to trust the person they are communicating with and feel a deeper connection with them. This type of open and honest communication is essential in building strong relationships, whether they are professional or personal.

Another important factor in building trust and connection is consistency. People are more likely to trust someone who is reliable and consistent in their actions and words. When someone says they will do something, and then follows through on that promise, it builds trust. Similarly, when individuals behave in a consistent manner and show that they can be relied upon, it helps to strengthen the connection between them. Consistency shows that a person is trustworthy and committed to the relationship, which is crucial in building trust and connection.

Building trust and connection also involves being authentic and vulnerable. People are more likely to trust and connect with someone who is genuine and who shares their true thoughts and feelings. When individuals are open and honest about who they are and what they believe, it helps to build a sense of authenticity and trust. Similarly, when individuals are willing to be vulnerable and share their weaknesses, fears, and struggles, it can help to deepen the connection between them. Vulnerability is a powerful tool in building trust and connection because it shows that a person is willing to let their guard down and be truly seen by others.

In addition to communication, consistency, authenticity, and vulnerability, building trust and connection also involves showing respect and empathy towards others. When individuals treat each other with respect and show empathy for their thoughts, feelings, and experiences, it helps to build a sense of trust and connection. Respect is essential in any relationship because it shows that individuals value and care for each other. Empathy, on the other hand, is the ability to understand and share the feelings of another person. When individuals show empathy towards others, it helps to build a deeper connection and trust. Trust is the foundation upon which all relationships are built, and without it, communication and collaboration become difficult. Connection, on the other hand, is the bond that forms between individuals when trust is established. By focusing on effective communication, consistency, authenticity, vulnerability, respect, and empathy, individuals can build trust and connection in their personal and professional relationships. Trust and connection are key ingredients in building strong and fulfilling relationships, and by prioritizing these factors, individuals can create deeper and more meaningful connections with others.

....

- IMPACT OF SOCIAL MEDIA on Teenage Behavior

Social media has become an integral part of the daily lives of teenagers around the world. With the rise of platforms such as Instagram, Snapchat, and TikTok, young people are constantly connected to their peers and the wider online community. While social media has many benefits, such as facilitating communication and fostering creativity, it also has a profound impact on teenage behavior. In this essay, we will explore the various ways in which social media influences the behavior of teenagers, both positively and negatively.

One of the most significant ways in which social media affects teenage behavior is through its impact on self-esteem and body image. With the prevalence of filters and editing tools on social media platforms, teenagers are constantly exposed to images of seemingly flawless individuals. This can lead to feelings of inadequacy and lower self-esteem among teenagers, as they compare themselves to these unrealistic standards. Additionally, the culture of likes and followers on social media can create a sense of validation based on external factors, rather than on one's intrinsic worth. This can lead to a constant quest for approval and validation from others, which can have a detrimental effect on a teenager's mental health.

Furthermore, social media has been linked to an increase in feelings of anxiety and depression among teenagers. The constant barrage of information and images on social media can be overwhelming, leading to heightened levels of stress and anxiety. Additionally, cyberbullying has become a prevalent issue on social media platforms, as teenagers can hide behind the anonymity of a screen to harass and intimidate their peers. This can have a lasting impact on a teenager's mental health and well-being, leading to feelings of isolation and depression. It is important for parents and educators to be aware of these risks and to provide support and guidance to teenagers who may be struggling with their mental health due to social media.

On the other hand, social media can also have positive effects on teenage behavior. For example, social media can be a valuable tool for learning and self-expression. Teenagers can use social media platforms to connect with like-minded individuals, share their passions and interests, and even learn new skills. Additionally, social media can be a powerful platform for activism and social change, as teenagers can raise awareness about important issues and mobilize their peers to take action. By harnessing the power of social media for positive purposes, teenagers can make a difference in their communities and beyond. While social media can foster connections and creativity, it can also lead to feelings of inadequacy, anxiety, and depression among teenagers. It is important for parents, educators, and policymakers to be aware of the risks associated with social media and to provide support and guidance to teenagers who may be struggling with their mental health as a result. By promoting responsible and balanced use of social media, we can help teenagers navigate this digital landscape in a healthy and positive way.

- Online Safety and Cyberbullying

Online safety and cyberbullying have become increasingly important topics in today's digital age. With the widespread use of the internet and social media platforms, individuals of all ages are at risk of encountering cyberbullying and online threats. It is essential for individuals to be aware of the risks and take proactive steps to protect themselves and others online.

One of the key aspects of online safety is understanding how to protect personal information and privacy online. This includes being cautious about the information shared on social media platforms and ensuring that privacy settings are set to the highest level. Cyberbullies often target individuals who share personal information online, as this information can be used to harass or intimidate the individual. By being mindful of the information shared online, individuals can reduce the risk of becoming a target for cyberbullying.

In addition to protecting personal information, individuals should also be cautious when interacting with others online. Cyberbullies often use social media platforms and messaging apps to harass and intimidate others. It is important for individuals to be aware of the signs of cyberbullying, such as receiving threatening or harassing messages, having fake accounts created in their name, or being publicly shamed or humiliated online. If individuals experience cyberbullying, they should report the behavior to the platform in question and reach out to a trusted adult or professional for support.

Education and awareness are key components of preventing cyberbullying and promoting online safety. School programs and community organizations should offer resources and information to educate individuals about the risks of cyberbullying and how to protect themselves online. By raising awareness about cyberbullying and online safety, individuals can make informed decisions about their online behavior and take steps to protect themselves and others from harm.

It is also important for parents and caregivers to be involved in their children's online activities and help them navigate the complexities of the digital world. Parents should actively monitor their children's online interactions and set guidelines for safe internet usage. By discussing online safety and cyberbullying with their children, parents can empower them to make smart choices and seek help if they encounter harmful behavior online. By understanding the risks of cyberbullying and taking proactive steps to protect personal information and privacy online, individuals can reduce their risk of becoming a target for cyberbullying. Education, awareness, and communication are key in promoting online safety and preventing cyberbullying. By working together as a community to address these issues, we can create a safer and more positive online environment for all individuals.

- Screen Time and Healthy Habits

In today's modern society, the proliferation of technology has led to an increase in screen time for individuals of all ages. From smartphones to tablets to computers, screens have become an integral part of our daily lives. While the convenience and efficiency of technology cannot be denied, the excessive use of screens can have negative impacts on our overall health and well-being. It is important for individuals to be mindful of their screen time and to develop healthy habits to ensure a balanced and fulfilling lifestyle.

One of the key concerns associated with excessive screen time is the impact on physical health. Prolonged use of screens can lead to a sedentary lifestyle, as individuals often sit for extended periods of time while engaging with technology. This lack of physical activity can contribute to weight gain, muscle stiffness, and poor posture. Additionally, staring at screens for long periods of time can strain the eyes and cause symptoms such as dryness, headaches, and blurred vision. In order to mitigate these negative effects, it is important for individuals to take regular breaks from screens, engage in physical activity, and practice good ergonomics while using technology.

In addition to physical health concerns, excessive screen time can also have a negative impact on mental health. Studies have shown that prolonged use of screens, especially before bedtime, can disrupt sleep patterns and lead to poor quality sleep. This can result in fatigue, irritability, and difficulty concentrating during the day. Furthermore, the constant stimulation from screens can contribute to feelings of anxiety and depression. To promote better mental health, individuals should establish a bedtime routine that does not involve screens, engage in relaxation techniques such as meditation or deep breathing, and prioritize face-to-face interactions with loved ones.

Another area of concern related to screen time is the impact on social relationships. The prevalence of social media and online communication has made it easier for individuals to stay connected, but it has also led to a decrease in meaningful face-to-face interactions. Excessive use of screens can lead to feelings of isolation, loneliness, and disconnection from others. To foster healthier relationships, individuals should make an effort to limit their screen time and focus on quality interactions with friends and family members. This can involve setting boundaries for technology use, scheduling regular in-person gatherings, and engaging in activities that promote bonding and connection.

While it is important to be mindful of the negative effects of excessive screen time, it is also essential to recognize the positive aspects that technology can bring to our lives. Screens can be powerful tools for communication, education, and entertainment. They can connect us to information from around the world, facilitate remote work and learning, and provide endless opportunities for creativity and self-expression. By striking a balance between screen time and healthy habits, individuals can harness the benefits of technology while also prioritizing their physical, mental, and social well-being. By being mindful of our technology use and establishing healthy habits, we can ensure that screens enhance, rather than hinder, our quality of life. It is essential for individuals to take breaks from screens, prioritize physical activity and good ergonomics, establish a bedtime routine that does not involve screens, engage in relaxation techniques, and focus on quality face-to-face interactions.

By adopting these practices, we can enjoy the benefits of technology while also promoting a balanced and fulfilling lifestyle.

Chapter 5: School, Academics, and Goals

• • • •

- MOTIVATING TEENAGERS towards Academic Success

Motivating teenagers towards academic success is a crucial aspect of their development and future prospects. Teenagers often face numerous challenges and distractions that may hinder their academic progress, such as peer pressure, social media, and personal issues. However, it is essential to understand the importance of instilling a strong sense of motivation in teenagers to help them achieve their academic goals and excel in their studies.

One of the key factors in motivating teenagers towards academic success is setting clear and achievable goals. By establishing realistic academic goals, teenagers are more likely to stay focused and motivated to succeed. These goals should be specific, measurable, and attainable, allowing teenagers to track their progress and see the tangible results of their efforts. Encouraging teenagers to set both short-term and long-term goals can help them stay motivated and committed to their academic pursuits.

Another effective way to motivate teenagers towards academic success is through positive reinforcement and praise. By acknowledging and celebrating their achievements, teenagers are more likely to feel valued and encouraged to continue working hard. Whether it is a high grade on a test or completing a challenging assignment, recognizing their efforts and accomplishments can boost their confidence and motivation to excel academically. Additionally, providing constructive feedback and guidance can help teenagers improve their academic performance and strive for greater success.

In addition to setting goals and providing positive reinforcement, fostering a supportive and nurturing environment can also motivate teenagers towards academic success. Encouraging open communication and creating a sense of community within the academic setting can provide teenagers with the resources and support they need to thrive academically. By building strong relationships with teachers, mentors, and peers, teenagers can receive the encouragement and guidance necessary to overcome obstacles and achieve their academic goals.

Furthermore, helping teenagers develop a growth mindset can significantly impact their motivation towards academic success. By promoting the belief that intelligence and abilities can be developed through hard work and perseverance, teenagers are more likely to embrace challenges and view setbacks as opportunities for growth. Encouraging teenagers to adopt a growth mindset can empower them to take risks, learn from failures, and continuously strive for personal and academic improvement. By instilling a sense of motivation and determination in teenagers, we can empower them to overcome obstacles, achieve their academic goals, and realize their full potential. Through fostering a culture of academic excellence and providing the necessary support and guidance, we can help teenagers navigate the challenges of adolescence and succeed in their academic endeavors.

- Balancing Extracurricular Activities

Balancing extracurricular activities is a crucial aspect of a student's overall academic and personal development. Engaging in extracurricular activities not only provides students with opportunities to explore their interests and passions outside of the classroom but also enhances their interpersonal skills, time management, and leadership abilities. However, finding the right balance between academics and extracurriculars can be challenging for many students. It is essential for students to understand the importance of prioritizing their commitments and managing their time effectively to ensure they can excel in both their academic and extracurricular pursuits.

One of the key factors in balancing extracurricular activities is time management. Students must learn to effectively allocate their time between academic responsibilities, extracurricular activities, and personal commitments. This requires careful planning and organization to ensure that they are able to meet deadlines and fulfill their obligations in all aspects of their lives. Setting realistic goals and creating a schedule or timetable can help students stay on track and make the most of their time. It is important for students to prioritize their tasks based on urgency and importance, and to allocate sufficient time for studying, completing assignments, attending classes, and participating in extracurricular activities.

Another important aspect of balancing extracurricular activities is prioritization. Students must learn to prioritize their commitments and make choices based on their values and goals. While it can be tempting to join multiple clubs and organizations, it is crucial for students to be selective in order to avoid spreading themselves too thin. By prioritizing their extracurricular activities based on their interests, skills, and career aspirations, students can make the most of their experiences and maximize their impact. It is important for students to evaluate their commitments regularly and make adjustments as needed to ensure they are able to focus on their most important priorities.

Furthermore, effective communication is essential in balancing extracurricular activities. Students must learn to communicate with their teachers, advisors, coaches, and peers to keep them informed of their commitments and seek support when needed. Clear and open communication can help students manage their responsibilities more effectively and prevent misunderstandings or conflicts from arising. By maintaining open lines of communication with all relevant parties, students can ensure that they are able to fulfill their obligations and receive the necessary support to succeed in both their academic and extracurricular pursuits.

In addition, it is important for students to set boundaries and practice self-care in order to maintain balance in their lives. While extracurricular activities can be enriching and rewarding, it is crucial for students to prioritize their well-being and avoid overextending themselves. Setting boundaries and taking time to rest, relax, and recharge is essential for maintaining physical and mental health. Students should also be mindful of their own limits and know when to say no to additional commitments in order to avoid burnout. By practicing self-care and prioritizing their well-being, students can ensure that they are able to maintain a healthy balance between their academic and extracurricular pursuits. By practicing effective time management, prioritization, communication, and self-care, students can successfully navigate their commitments and excel in both their academic and extracurricular pursuits. It is important for students to be mindful of their goals and values, and to make choices that align with their interests and aspirations. By finding the right balance between academics and extracurriculars, students can gain valuable skills, experiences, and connections that will benefit them throughout their academic and professional careers.

- College and Career Planning

College and career planning are essential components of a successful future. By carefully considering your interests, strengths, and goals, you can create a roadmap that will guide you towards a fulfilling and rewarding career. It's important to start this process early on in your academic journey, as it can help you make informed choices about your education and career path. Whether you're a high school student just beginning to explore your options or a college student looking to make a career change, taking the time to develop a solid plan can set you up for long-term success.

One of the first steps in college and career planning is to assess your interests, skills, and values. This self-assessment can help you understand what kind of career path might be a good fit for you. Consider what subjects you enjoy studying, activities you excel at, and values that are important to you. This information can help you narrow down your options and identify potential career paths that align with your strengths and interests. Some useful tools for self-assessment include career aptitude tests, personality assessments, and informational interviews with professionals in fields you're interested in.

Once you have a better understanding of your interests and strengths, it's time to research potential career paths and college programs that align with your goals. Look into the job market for different industries, the educational requirements for various careers, and the earning potential for different fields. Consider meeting with a career counselor or academic advisor to get personalized guidance on your options. Additionally, explore different colleges and universities to see what programs they offer and what resources they provide for career planning. It's important to choose a college or university that will support your academic and career goals and provide you with the necessary resources to succeed.

As you consider different career paths and educational programs, it's important to think about your long-term goals and how they align with your values and lifestyle preferences. Consider what kind of work environment you thrive in, what kind of work-life balance you desire, and what your financial goals are. By thinking about these factors upfront, you can ensure that you're making informed decisions about your education and career path. Additionally, consider how different career paths align with your personal values and passions. Choosing a career that aligns with your values can lead to greater job satisfaction and overall fulfillment in your professional life.

Once you have a solid understanding of your interests, goals, and values, it's time to create a concrete plan for achieving your career goals. This plan should include short-term goals (such as completing specific courses or gaining relevant work experience) as well as long-term goals (such as obtaining a specific degree or certification or reaching a certain level of expertise in your field). Consider what steps you need to take to achieve these goals, what resources you'll need to access, and what potential obstacles you might encounter along the way. By creating a detailed plan, you can stay focused and motivated as you work towards your career goals.

In addition to creating a plan for your career goals, it's important to seek out opportunities for experiential learning and professional development. This can include internships, volunteer work, part-time jobs, or extracurricular activities that allow you to gain relevant skills and experience in your field of interest. These opportunities can not only help you build your resume and gain practical experience, but they can also help you clarify your career goals and make informed decisions about your future. Additionally, consider seeking out mentors or professionals in your field who can provide guidance and support as you navigate your career path.

To wrap up, it's important to remain flexible and adaptable as you navigate your college and career planning process. Career paths can change, goals can shift, and unexpected opportunities can arise. By remaining open to new possibilities and willing to make adjustments to your plan as needed, you can ensure that you're able to adapt to changing circumstances and continue moving towards your long-term goals. Remember that college and career planning is an ongoing process, and it's important to regularly reassess your goals and progress to ensure that you're on track to achieving your desired career outcomes. By approaching the college and career planning process with intentionality, flexibility, and determination, you can set yourself up for a successful and fulfilling future.

....

- UNDERSTANDING THE risks of Alcohol and Drugs

Alcohol and drugs are substances that have been used throughout history for various reasons, such as relaxation, socialization, and recreation. However, it is important to understand the risks associated with their use in order to make informed decisions about their consumption. Both alcohol and drugs can have negative effects on our physical, mental, and emotional well-being if used improperly or in excess.

One of the primary risks of alcohol consumption is the potential for addiction. Alcohol is a depressant that affects the central nervous system, and over time, regular consumption can lead to physical dependence. This can result in withdrawal symptoms such as tremors, sweating, and anxiety when a person tries to stop drinking. In severe cases, alcohol addiction can lead to serious health problems such as liver disease, heart disease, and neurological disorders. It can also have a negative impact on relationships, work performance, and overall quality of life.

Similarly, drugs can also be addictive and can have a range of negative effects on the body and mind. Drugs can alter brain function and chemistry, leading to changes in mood, behavior, and cognitive abilities. They can also cause physical harm to the body, such as damage to the heart, lungs, and liver. Drug addiction can have devastating consequences on a person's life, leading to financial problems, legal issues, and strained relationships with family and friends.

In addition to the risks of addiction, alcohol and drugs can impair judgment and decision-making abilities, leading to risky behaviors and accidents. Alcohol, in particular, is a common factor in motor vehicle accidents, violence, and other dangerous situations. Drugs can also impair coordination and cognitive function, increasing the risk of accidents and injuries. It is important to be aware of the effects of these substances on our ability to function safely and responsibly in our daily lives.

Another important risk of alcohol and drug use is the potential for overdose. Both alcohol and drugs can be toxic to the body in high doses, leading to overdose and potential death. Overdose symptoms can vary depending on the substance involved, but may include respiratory depression, seizures, and loss of consciousness. It is important to be aware of the signs of overdose and seek medical help immediately if you suspect that someone has ingested a dangerous amount of alcohol or drugs. Addiction, impaired judgment, accidents, and overdose are just a few of the potential dangers of using these substances. By educating ourselves and others about the risks of alcohol and drugs, we can help prevent harm and promote healthier lifestyles. Remember to always drink alcohol and use drugs responsibly, and seek help if you or someone you know is struggling with addiction.

- Identifying Warning Signs of Substance Abuse

Substance abuse is a complex and serious issue that affects individuals of all ages and backgrounds. It can have devastating effects on a person's physical and mental health, as well as their relationships and overall well-being. Identifying warning signs of substance abuse is crucial in order to intervene early and prevent further harm.

One of the most common warning signs of substance abuse is a noticeable change in behavior. This can manifest as mood swings, irritability, and increased aggressiveness. Individuals may also begin to isolate themselves from friends and family, lose interest in activities they once enjoyed, and experience a decline in performance at school or work. These changes in behavior may be accompanied by secretive or evasive behavior, such as lying or making excuses for their actions.

Physical signs of substance abuse can also be telling. Individuals may exhibit changes in their physical appearance, such as unexplained weight loss or gain, poor hygiene, and bloodshot eyes. They may also experience frequent illnesses or infections, as substance abuse can weaken the immune system. Additionally, individuals may display tremors, slurred speech, or coordination problems, which can be indicative of substance intoxication.

Another common warning sign of substance abuse is a preoccupation with obtaining and using drugs or alcohol. Individuals may spend excessive amounts of time and money on their substance of choice, and may sacrifice important obligations in order to maintain their habit. They may also exhibit a lack of motivation and drive, as their focus shifts increasingly towards their substance use. This can lead to financial difficulties, legal issues, and strained relationships with loved ones.

In addition to behavioral and physical signs, there are also emotional warning signs of substance abuse. Individuals may experience intense mood swings, ranging from euphoria and exaggerated confidence to depression and apathy. They may also exhibit signs of anxiety or paranoia, and may have difficulty regulating their emotions. Substance abuse can exacerbate underlying mental health issues, making it important to address both issues simultaneously.

It is important to note that not all warning signs will be present in every case of substance abuse. Some individuals may exhibit only a few warning signs, while others may display a combination of multiple signs. It is also important to consider the context in which these signs occur, as some changes in behavior or physical appearance may have other explanations unrelated to substance abuse.

If you suspect that someone you know is struggling with substance abuse, it is important to approach the situation with compassion and empathy. Encourage open communication, and offer your support without judgment. Help them to seek professional help, whether that be through therapy, counseling, or a rehabilitation program. Remember that substance abuse is a complex issue with no easy solutions, and that recovery is a journey that may require time and patience. By recognizing changes in behavior, physical appearance, and emotions, as well as a preoccupation with substance use, we can provide support and guidance to those who are struggling. Approach the situation with compassion and empathy, and encourage the individual to seek help from a professional. With early intervention and support, we can help individuals overcome substance abuse and live healthier, happier lives.

- Intervention and Support

Intervention and support are essential components of effective strategies for addressing a wide range of issues facing individuals and communities.

Whether it is a personal struggle with mental health challenges, a family in crisis, or a community grappling with the impacts of poverty and inequality, interventions and support systems play a crucial role in providing assistance and promoting positive outcomes. In this discussion, we will explore the key principles of intervention and support, the various forms they can take, and their importance in promoting well-being and resilience.

At its core, intervention refers to intentional actions taken to address a specific issue or problem. This can involve providing support, resources, or guidance to individuals or groups in need. Interventions can take many forms, ranging from individual counseling and therapy to community-based programs and policies aimed at addressing social determinants of health and well-being. The goal of intervention is to intervene in a situation to prevent further harm or negative outcomes, and to promote positive change and growth.

Support, on the other hand, is the provision of assistance, encouragement, or resources to help individuals or groups navigate challenges and achieve their goals. Support can be emotional, financial, or practical in nature, and can come from a variety of sources, including friends, family, community organizations, and professional service providers. Support systems are crucial for building resilience and coping with adversity, as they provide a network of resources and connections that can help individuals overcome obstacles and thrive in the face of adversity.

Intervention and support are closely linked, as interventions often involve providing support to individuals or groups in need. For example, a mental health intervention may include connecting individuals with supportive services such as counseling, peer support groups, or medication management. Similarly, a community-based intervention aimed at reducing poverty and inequality may involve providing resources and support to families in need, such as job training, affordable housing, or access to healthcare services. By combining targeted interventions with comprehensive support systems, we can address complex issues in a holistic and sustainable way.

There are many different approaches to intervention and support, depending on the nature of the issue and the needs of the individuals or communities involved. Some interventions focus on crisis management and immediate stabilization, such as providing emergency shelter to individuals experiencing homelessness or counseling services to individuals in acute psychological distress. Other interventions are more long-term and preventive in nature, such as early childhood education programs, job training initiatives, or community-based health promotion efforts.

Regardless of the specific approach, effective intervention and support strategies share some common principles. First and foremost, interventions should be evidence-based and tailored to the needs of the individuals or communities they are intended to serve. This may involve conducting thorough assessments to identify underlying issues and developing customized plans that address multiple dimensions of well-being, such as physical health, mental health, social connections, and economic stability. Interventions should also be culturally competent and sensitive to the unique experiences and strengths of the individuals or communities they are serving.

Another key principle of effective intervention and support is collaboration and partnership. No single individual or organization can address complex issues alone, which is why collaboration among multiple stakeholders is essential for success. This may involve forming partnerships with community-based organizations, government agencies, academic institutions, and private sector entities to leverage resources, expertise, and networks of support. By working together in a coordinated and integrated manner, we can maximize the impact of interventions and support efforts and achieve more sustainable and equitable outcomes for all involved. By providing targeted interventions and comprehensive support systems, we can help individuals and communities overcome challenges, build resilience, and achieve their full potential. Effective intervention and support strategies are evidence-based, culturally competent, and collaborative in nature, and are grounded in a deep understanding of the unique needs and strengths of the individuals or communities they are intended to serve. By embracing these principles and working together in a spirit of partnership and solidarity, we can create a more just and compassionate society where everyone has the opportunity to thrive.

. . . .

- PUBERTY AND PHYSICAL Changes

Puberty is a crucial stage in human development that marks the transition from childhood to adulthood. It is a period of rapid physical, emotional, and cognitive changes that occur in both boys and girls. During puberty, the body undergoes a series of transformations that prepare an individual for reproductive maturity.

One of the most significant physical changes that occur during puberty is the development of secondary sexual characteristics. In boys, these changes include the growth of facial and body hair, deepening of the voice, and an increase in muscle mass. In girls, puberty brings about the development of breast tissue, the onset of menstruation, and the growth of pubic hair. These changes are driven by the increased production of hormones such as testosterone in boys and estrogen in girls.

The timing of puberty varies among individuals and can be influenced by a variety of factors, including genetics, nutrition, and overall health. In general, girls tend to enter puberty earlier than boys, with the onset of physical changes typically occurring between the ages of 8 and 13. Boys, on the other hand, typically begin puberty between the ages of 10 and 15. However, it is important to note that these are just general guidelines, and there is a wide range of normal variation in the timing of puberty.

In addition to the development of secondary sexual characteristics, puberty also brings about changes in growth and body composition. During puberty, both boys and girls experience a significant growth spurt, with boys typically reaching their peak height velocity around the age of 14 and girls reaching theirs around the age of 12. This rapid growth is accompanied by changes in body shape, with boys developing broader shoulders and a narrower waist, while girls develop wider hips and a more pronounced curve in their lower back.

Puberty also has a profound impact on the mind and emotions of adolescents. The hormonal changes that occur during puberty can lead to mood swings, increased irritability, and heightened emotional reactivity. Adolescents may also experience changes in their self-image and self-esteem as they navigate the physical changes that come with puberty. It is important for parents, teachers, and other adults to be supportive and understanding during this time, as adolescents may be feeling insecure or self-conscious about their changing bodies. It is a time of rapid physical, emotional, and cognitive changes that can be challenging for adolescents to navigate. By providing them with support, understanding, and accurate information about the changes they are experiencing, we can help adolescents navigate this crucial stage of development with confidence and resilience.

- Promoting Positive Body Image

Promoting positive body image is a crucial aspect of mental and emotional well-being for individuals of all ages and backgrounds. In today's society, there is an immense amount of pressure and influence to adhere to unrealistic beauty standards that can have detrimental effects on one's self-esteem and self-worth. These standards are perpetuated through various forms of media, advertising, and social interactions, leading many to feel insecure about their bodies and appearance. It is essential to address and combat these harmful messages by promoting a more inclusive and accepting definition of beauty that celebrates diversity and individuality.

One of the key ways to promote positive body image is through education and awareness. By providing individuals with accurate information about body image, self-esteem, and the impact of media and societal pressures, we can empower them to challenge and resist harmful messages. This can be done through school programs, workshops, and community initiatives that promote body positivity and self-acceptance. Additionally, healthcare providers and mental health professionals can play a crucial role in promoting positive body image by addressing body image concerns with their patients and providing them with tools and resources to improve their self-esteem.

Another important aspect of promoting positive body image is by fostering a culture of kindness and acceptance. By promoting kindness and compassion towards oneself and others, we can create a more supportive and inclusive environment that values diversity and individuality. This can be done by promoting positive self-talk, practicing self-care, and cultivating healthy relationships with others that prioritize respect and acceptance. Additionally, promoting media literacy and critical thinking skills can help individuals to recognize and challenge harmful beauty standards and unrealistic portrayals of beauty.

Furthermore, promoting positive body image also involves advocating for policy and societal changes that promote inclusivity and diversity. This can include supporting campaigns and initiatives that challenge harmful beauty standards, promoting diversity in representation in media and advertising, and advocating for policies that protect individuals from discrimination based on their appearance. By creating a more inclusive and accepting society, we can help individuals to feel confident and comfortable in their own skin, regardless of their size, shape, or appearance. By raising awareness, fostering kindness and acceptance, and advocating for policy and societal changes, we can work towards creating a more inclusive and accepting society that celebrates diversity and individuality. It is important for all individuals to recognize and challenge harmful beauty standards and unrealistic portrayals of beauty, and to prioritize self-acceptance and self-love. By promoting positive body image, we can help individuals to feel confident, empowered, and comfortable in their own skin.

- Boosting Self-Esteem and Confidence

Self-esteem and confidence play a crucial role in an individual's overall well-being and success. They are essential components of a person's mental health and have a significant impact on their ability to navigate through life's challenges. Boosting self-esteem and confidence is a goal that many people strive to achieve, as it can lead to increased happiness, resilience, and motivation.

One of the key ways to boost self-esteem and confidence is through self-awareness and self-acceptance. This involves recognizing your strengths and weaknesses, as well as accepting yourself for who you are. By acknowledging your positive qualities and accomplishments, you can build a stronger sense of self-worth and belief in your abilities. Additionally, being kind and compassionate towards yourself, rather than engaging in self-criticism or negative self-talk, can help to foster a more positive self-image.

Setting realistic goals and taking steps towards achieving them is another effective way to boost self-esteem and confidence. By setting specific, achievable goals, you can build a sense of accomplishment and progress, which can help to increase your self-confidence. Breaking down larger goals into smaller tasks can also help to make them more manageable and less daunting. Celebrating your successes, no matter how small, can further reinforce your sense of self-worth and confidence.

Another important aspect of boosting self-esteem and confidence is cultivating positive relationships and social support. Surrounding yourself with people who uplift and support you can help to build your confidence and self-esteem. Having a strong support system can provide validation and encouragement, which can help to counteract any negative self-perceptions. Additionally, engaging in activities and hobbies that bring you joy and fulfillment can help to boost your self-esteem and confidence by providing a sense of purpose and belonging.

Practicing self-care and prioritizing your physical and mental well-being are also essential for boosting self-esteem and confidence. Taking care of your body through regular exercise, healthy eating, and proper rest can help to improve your overall sense of self-worth and confidence. Additionally, engaging in activities that promote relaxation and stress relief, such as meditation or mindfulness practices, can help to improve your mental health and well-being. Prioritizing self-care can help to increase your confidence and resilience, allowing you to face challenges and setbacks with a positive mindset.

Developing and honing your skills and talents can also be instrumental in boosting self-esteem and confidence. Investing time and effort in activities and pursuits that you are passionate about can help to build your self-confidence and sense of accomplishment. By continually learning and growing, you can increase your self-esteem and confidence by expanding your knowledge and abilities. Additionally, seeking feedback and guidance from others can help to improve your skills and increase your confidence in your abilities. By cultivating self-awareness, setting realistic goals, building positive relationships, practicing self-care, and developing your skills and talents, you can increase your self-esteem and confidence and achieve greater happiness and success. Remember that building self-esteem and confidence is a journey that requires patience, dedication, and self-compassion. By taking small steps each day to enhance your self-esteem and confidence, you can create a more fulfilling and rewarding life for yourself.

Chapter 8: Relationships and Dating

• • • •

- HEALTHY VS. UNHEALTHY Relationships

Relationships are an essential aspect of human life, providing connection, support, and companionship. However, not all relationships are created equal. Some relationships are healthy and contribute positively to our well-being, while others are unhealthy and can have a negative impact on our mental and emotional health. It is important to be able to distinguish between healthy and unhealthy relationships in order to cultivate and maintain positive and fulfilling connections with others.

Healthy relationships are characterized by mutual respect, trust, communication, and support. In a healthy relationship, both individuals feel valued and respected, and their opinions and feelings are taken into consideration. Trust is a key component of a healthy relationship, as both individuals feel secure and can rely on each other. Communication is another vital aspect of a healthy relationship, where both individuals are able to express their thoughts, feelings, and needs openly and honestly. Support is also crucial in a healthy relationship, as both individuals are there for each other during times of need and celebrate each other's successes.

On the other hand, unhealthy relationships are characterized by a lack of respect, trust, communication, and support. In an unhealthy relationship, one or both individuals may feel controlled, manipulated, or belittled by the other. Trust may be lacking, leading to insecurity and doubts about the other person's intentions. Communication may be ineffective or even abusive, with one or both individuals unable to express themselves openly and honestly. Support may be lacking or conditional, with one individual only offering help when it benefits them or using support as a means of control.

Recognizing the signs of an unhealthy relationship is important in order to protect our well-being and avoid unnecessary harm. Some red flags of an unhealthy relationship include:

- Lack of respect: If one or both individuals do not value or respect each other's boundaries, opinions, or feelings, it can lead to a toxic environment where one person feels diminished or unimportant.

- Lack of trust: If there is constant doubt, suspicion, or jealousy in a relationship, it can erode trust and lead to feelings of insecurity and anxiety.

- Poor communication: If one or both individuals are unable to express themselves openly and honestly, it can lead to misunderstandings, conflicts, and resentment.

- Lack of support: If one individual is always giving and the other is always taking, or if support is only provided when it benefits one individual, it can create an imbalance and lead to feelings of resentment and dissatisfaction.

In order to cultivate healthy relationships, it is important to set boundaries, communicate effectively, and seek support when needed. Setting boundaries allows us to establish clear expectations and limits in our relationships, ensuring that our needs and well-being are respected. Effective communication helps us express ourselves openly and honestly, allowing us to connect authentically with others and resolve conflicts constructively. Seeking support from friends, family, or a therapist can also help us navigate challenges and strengthen our relationships. By recognizing the signs of an unhealthy relationship and taking steps to cultivate healthy connections, we can protect our well-being and foster positive and fulfilling relationships with others. In doing so, we can enhance our mental and emotional health and experience greater happiness and satisfaction in our interactions with others.

- Teaching Consent and Boundaries

Teaching consent and boundaries is an essential component of education, particularly in today's society where conversations around consent and healthy relationships are becoming increasingly important. By teaching students about consent and boundaries, we equip them with the knowledge and skills to navigate interpersonal relationships in a respectful and ethical manner. This not only helps to prevent instances of sexual misconduct and harassment but also promotes a culture of mutual respect and understanding.

One of the key concepts that students need to understand when it comes to consent is that it is a voluntary agreement between individuals to engage in sexual activity. This means that consent must be given freely, willingly, and enthusiastically, without any form of coercion or pressure. It is crucial for students to understand that consent is not just the absence of a "no" but rather an affirmative, ongoing, and mutual dialogue between partners. By emphasizing the importance of enthusiastic consent, we empower students to advocate for their boundaries and communicate their desires effectively.

In addition to understanding what consent is, students also need to be taught about the different forms that consent can take. This includes verbal, non-verbal, and enthusiastic consent, as well as the importance of respecting boundaries and recognizing signs of discomfort. By educating students about these different forms of consent, we help them to develop a more nuanced understanding of how consent operates in real-life situations and empower them to make informed decisions about their own relationships.

Teaching boundaries is another crucial aspect of promoting healthy relationships and preventing instances of harm. Boundaries are the limits that individuals set for themselves in order to protect their physical, emotional, and mental well-being. By teaching students about boundaries, we help them to recognize and respect their own boundaries as well as those of others. This includes understanding the importance of consent in all interactions, not just sexual ones, and learning to communicate their boundaries clearly and assertively.

When teaching consent and boundaries, it is important to create a safe and inclusive learning environment where students feel comfortable discussing sensitive topics. This can be achieved by establishing ground rules for respectful communication, setting clear expectations for behavior, and providing resources for students who may need additional support. It is also important to approach these topics with sensitivity and empathy, recognizing that students may have different backgrounds and experiences that shape their understanding of consent and boundaries.

In addition to formal instruction in the classroom, it is also important to integrate conversations about consent and boundaries into everyday interactions and activities. This can include incorporating discussions about consent into literature, history, and social studies lessons, as well as creating opportunities for students to practice setting boundaries in role-playing scenarios or group discussions. By reinforcing these concepts in multiple contexts, we help students to internalize the importance of consent and boundaries as fundamental principles of healthy relationships. By equipping students with the knowledge and skills to navigate interpersonal relationships ethically and responsibly, we empower them to create positive and supportive communities where all individuals feel safe and valued. Through continued education and open dialogue, we can work towards building a society where consent is understood, respected, and practiced in all interactions.

- Supportive Parenting in Teenage Relationships

Supportive parenting in teenage relationships is a crucial component in promoting healthy adolescent development. Adolescence is a period of rapid physical, emotional, and cognitive changes, and teenagers often rely on the guidance and support of their parents to navigate the complexities of romantic relationships. Supportive parenting involves providing teens with the tools, resources, and emotional support they need to build and maintain healthy relationships. This type of parenting fosters trust, open communication, and respect within the parent-teen relationship, which in turn helps teenagers develop the skills they need to form and maintain positive relationships with their peers.

One of the key aspects of supportive parenting in teenage relationships is communication. Parents who engage in open and honest communication with their teens create a safe space for them to discuss their feelings, concerns, and experiences. By actively listening to their teens and validating their emotions, parents can help them develop the self-awareness and emotional intelligence needed to navigate the challenges of teen relationships. Additionally, parents can use communication as a tool to educate their teens about healthy relationship behaviors and boundaries, helping them make informed decisions about their romantic partners.

Another important aspect of supportive parenting in teenage relationships is setting boundaries and expectations. Establishing clear rules and guidelines for dating can help teens understand what is expected of them in a relationship and promote respect for themselves and their partners. By setting limits on time spent with a romantic partner, curfews, and appropriate behavior, parents can teach their teens the importance of healthy boundaries and mutual respect. Additionally, parents can model positive relationship behaviors in their own interactions, showing their teens what a healthy, respectful relationship looks like.

Supportive parenting in teenage relationships also involves providing teens with emotional support and guidance. Teenagers may experience intense emotions during their first romantic relationships, and parents can help them navigate these feelings by offering empathy, reassurance, and advice. By being available to listen and offer support when needed, parents can help their teens build resilience and coping skills that will serve them well in future relationships. Parents can also help their teens develop a healthy sense of self-worth and self-esteem, which can protect them from entering into unhealthy or abusive relationships.

In addition to emotional support, parents can provide practical guidance to help their teens build healthy relationships. This may involve teaching teens how to communicate effectively, resolve conflicts, and make decisions that are in their best interest. Parents can also help their teens learn how to set and respect boundaries, recognize signs of unhealthy behavior in their partners, and seek help if they find themselves in a difficult or potentially dangerous situation. By equipping their teens with these skills, parents can empower them to make informed choices about their relationships and build strong, supportive connections with their peers. By promoting open communication, setting boundaries and expectations, providing emotional support, and offering practical guidance, parents can help their teens build the skills and confidence they need to form and maintain positive relationships. By cultivating a supportive and nurturing environment within the parent-teen relationship, parents can help their teens navigate the complexities of teenage romance with grace and confidence, setting them up for success in their future relationships and beyond.

. . . .

- RECOGNIZING SIGNS of Mental Health Issues

Mental health issues affect millions of individuals worldwide and can have a significant impact on one's daily functioning and quality of life. It is crucial to recognize the signs of mental health issues early on so that individuals can receive the necessary support and treatment. By being aware of the signs and symptoms of various mental health conditions, individuals can take proactive steps to address their mental health needs and seek appropriate help.

One of the most common signs of mental health issues is changes in behavior. This can include sudden shifts in mood, increased irritability or anger, withdrawal from social activities, changes in eating or sleeping patterns, and difficulty concentrating. If someone you know is exhibiting these behavioral changes, it may be a sign that they are struggling with their mental health and may benefit from professional intervention. It's important to approach the individual with compassion and empathy, and to encourage them to seek help from a mental health professional.

Another key indicator of mental health issues is persistent feelings of sadness, hopelessness, or despair. It is normal to experience occasional feelings of sadness or low mood, but if these feelings persist for an extended period of time and interfere with one's ability to function, it may be a sign of depression or another mental health condition. Additionally, individuals who frequently express thoughts of self-harm or suicide should be taken seriously and provided with immediate support. If you or someone you know is experiencing these intense feelings, it is essential to reach out for help and seek treatment from a mental health provider.

Physical symptoms can also be signs of mental health issues. Chronic headaches, digestive issues, fatigue, and unexplained aches and pains can all be indicative of underlying mental health conditions such as anxiety or depression. It is important for individuals to pay attention to their physical symptoms and seek medical evaluation to rule out any underlying medical conditions. Seeking treatment for mental health issues can help alleviate physical symptoms and improve overall well-being.

Changes in cognition and thought patterns are additional signs of mental health issues. Individuals may experience racing thoughts, difficulty concentrating, memory problems, or irrational beliefs. These cognitive symptoms can significantly impact one's ability to perform daily tasks and interact with others. If you or someone you know is exhibiting these cognitive signs, it is vital to seek the guidance of a mental health professional who can provide support and appropriate intervention.

In addition to recognizing the signs of mental health issues in oneself or others, it is essential to understand that seeking help is a sign of strength, not weakness. There is no shame in reaching out for support for mental health concerns, and doing so can lead to improved emotional well-being and overall quality of life. Mental health professionals are trained to provide effective treatment for a wide range of mental health conditions, and therapy, medication, and other interventions can be instrumental in helping individuals manage their symptoms and lead fulfilling lives. By being aware of changes in behavior, mood, physical symptoms, cognition, and thought patterns, individuals can take proactive steps to address their mental health concerns and seek appropriate help. It is important to approach mental health issues with compassion, empathy, and understanding, and to encourage those who are struggling to reach out for support. Seeking help for mental health concerns is a sign of strength, and it can lead to improved quality of life and emotional well-being.

- Seeking Professional Help and Support

Seeking professional help and support is a crucial step in addressing and overcoming various challenges in life. Whether it be mental health issues, relationship problems, career dilemmas, or any other personal struggles, seeking help from a qualified professional can provide the guidance and support needed to navigate difficult situations and find solutions. While it may seem daunting or intimidating to reach out for help, it is important to remember that seeking assistance is a sign of strength and self-awareness.

One of the main reasons individuals may hesitate to seek professional help is due to stigma surrounding mental health and therapy. There is often a misconception that seeking help is a sign of weakness or failure, when in reality, it is a proactive and positive step towards self-improvement and growth. It takes courage and self-awareness to recognize when help is needed and to take the necessary steps to address issues that may be impacting one's well-being.

Another barrier to seeking professional help may be a lack of knowledge or understanding about the different types of support available. It can be overwhelming to navigate the various options for therapy, counseling, coaching, and other forms of professional help. However, by doing research, asking for recommendations, and reaching out to trusted sources, individuals can find the right type of support that best meets their needs and preferences.

It is also important to recognize that seeking professional help does not mean that one is giving up control or autonomy. In fact, it can empower individuals to take control of their lives and make positive changes. By working with a qualified professional, individuals can gain insights, tools, and strategies to address challenges, improve relationships, manage stress, and work towards their goals. Therapy and counseling sessions provide a safe and confidential space to explore thoughts and feelings, gain self-awareness, and develop coping skills.

In addition to individual therapy, group therapy can be a valuable source of support and validation. Group therapy allows individuals to connect with others who may be experiencing similar challenges, share experiences, and learn from each other's perspectives. It can provide a sense of community, belonging, and understanding that can be comforting and empowering. Group therapy can also help individuals build social skills, improve communication, and develop a support network of peers who can offer encouragement and empathy.

When seeking professional help, it is important to find a qualified and experienced professional who is a good fit for one's needs and preferences. This may involve researching different therapists, counselors, coaches, or support groups, reading reviews and testimonials, and asking for recommendations from friends, family, or healthcare providers. It is important to feel comfortable and safe with the professional, as the therapeutic relationship plays a crucial role in the effectiveness of the support and intervention. It is a sign of strength and self-awareness to recognize when help is needed and to take the necessary steps to address challenges and improve well-being. By working with a qualified professional, individuals can gain insights, tools, and strategies to navigate difficult situations, build resilience, and work towards their goals. Remember, you are not alone, and there is support available to help you on your journey towards healing and growth.

- Practicing Self-care and Coping Strategies

Self-care is a critical aspect of maintaining overall well-being and managing stress in today's fast-paced world. It is essential to prioritize self-care practices to ensure that we are able to function optimally in all aspects of our lives. Self-care encompasses a wide range of activities and strategies that help to promote physical, emotional, and mental well-being. By practicing self-care regularly, individuals can better cope with the challenges and demands of daily life.

One of the key components of self-care is taking care of our physical health. This includes getting enough sleep, eating a balanced diet, and engaging in regular physical activity. Adequate rest and proper nutrition are essential for maintaining energy levels and overall health. Regular exercise not only helps to improve physical fitness but also has been shown to have positive effects on mental health, such as reducing symptoms of anxiety and depression. By prioritizing physical health through proper self-care practices, individuals can enhance their overall well-being and resilience in the face of stress.

In addition to physical self-care, it is important to prioritize emotional and mental well-being through self-care practices. This can include mindfulness and relaxation techniques, such as meditation or deep breathing exercises, to help manage stress and promote emotional stability. Engaging in activities that bring joy and relaxation, such as reading a book, spending time with loved ones, or pursuing a hobby, can also help to reduce stress and improve emotional well-being. By incorporating these practices into our daily routine, we can better cope with the demands of daily life and maintain a sense of balance and perspective.

Another important aspect of self-care is setting boundaries and practicing self-compassion. It is important to recognize our limitations and prioritize our own needs in order to avoid burnout and maintain a healthy work-life balance. This may involve saying no to additional responsibilities or commitments when necessary, and providing ourselves with the time and space to rest and recharge.

Practicing self-compassion involves treating ourselves with kindness and understanding, particularly during times of stress or difficulty. By acknowledging our own needs and taking steps to meet them, we can better cope with the challenges of daily life and maintain a sense of well-being. By prioritizing physical, emotional, and mental health through self-care practices, individuals can enhance their resilience and ability to manage stress. Incorporating activities such as exercise, relaxation techniques, and setting boundaries can help to promote well-being and prevent burnout. By recognizing the importance of self-care and making it a priority in our daily lives, we can better cope with the challenges of modern life and maintain a sense of balance and perspective.

Chapter 10: Responsible Decision Making

• • • •

- TEACHING TEENAGERS about Consequences

Teaching teenagers about consequences is an essential aspect of their development and growth. Understanding consequences helps teenagers make informed decisions, take responsibility for their actions, and navigate the complexities of the world around them. By providing teenagers with the necessary tools and knowledge to comprehend the cause and effect relationship of their actions, educators and parents can empower them to make positive choices and avoid potentially harmful behaviors.

When teaching teenagers about consequences, it is important to emphasize the concept of accountability. Encouraging teenagers to take responsibility for their actions helps them understand the impact of their decisions on themselves and others. By instilling a sense of accountability, educators and parents can empower teenagers to think critically about the consequences of their choices and consider the long-term effects of their actions. This awareness can lead to increased self-awareness and empathy, as teenagers learn to recognize the significance of their behavior on those around them.

Additionally, teaching teenagers about consequences involves helping them understand the interconnected nature of cause and effect. By explaining how their actions can have both immediate and long-term repercussions, educators and parents can help teenagers develop a deeper understanding of the complexities of decision-making. This understanding can empower teenagers to think proactively about the consequences of their choices and consider the potential outcomes before making a decision. By fostering critical thinking skills and encouraging teenagers to think ahead, educators and parents can equip them with the tools needed to navigate the challenges of adolescence and beyond.

Incorporating real-life examples and scenarios into lessons about consequences can help teenagers better understand the concept in a practical and relatable way. By discussing actual situations and their outcomes, educators and parents can provide teenagers with concrete examples of the cause and effect relationship of their actions. This hands-on approach can help teenagers see the importance of considering the consequences of their choices and how different decisions can lead to varying outcomes. By making the concept of consequences tangible and relevant to teenagers' lives, educators and parents can help them internalize the importance of thinking before acting.

It is also important to create a safe and supportive environment for teenagers to learn about consequences. By fostering open communication and encouraging teenagers to ask questions, seek guidance, and share their thoughts and feelings, educators and parents can create a space where teenagers feel comfortable exploring complex issues and concepts. This open dialogue can help teenagers feel supported and understood as they navigate the challenges of adolescence and learn to make informed decisions. By cultivating a culture of trust and respect, educators and parents can empower teenagers to take ownership of their actions and embrace the lessons of consequences with confidence and maturity. By emphasizing the importance of accountability, cause and effect, real-life examples, and creating a safe and supportive environment, educators and parents can empower teenagers to make informed decisions, take responsibility for their actions, and navigate the complexities of the world around them. Through open communication, critical thinking skills, and practical learning experiences, teenagers can learn to consider the impact of their choices and make positive decisions that benefit themselves and those around them. By equipping teenagers with the necessary tools and knowledge to understand consequences, educators and parents can help them build a strong foundation for a successful and fulfilling future.

- Problem-solving Skills

Problem-solving skills are essential in both our personal and professional lives. These skills enable us to identify issues, analyze them, and come up with effective solutions. Developing strong problem-solving skills allows individuals to navigate challenges with confidence and effectively overcome obstacles to achieve their goals.

One key aspect of problem-solving skills is the ability to accurately identify the root causes of a problem. This involves carefully analyzing the situation and understanding the contributing factors that led to the issue at hand. By identifying the underlying causes of a problem, individuals can create targeted solutions that address the core issues rather than just treating the symptoms.

Critical thinking is another essential component of effective problem-solving. This involves the ability to evaluate information, make connections, and draw logical s. Critical thinking helps individuals to consider all angles of a problem, weigh the potential outcomes of different solutions, and make informed decisions. By honing their critical thinking skills, individuals can approach problems in a systematic and logical manner, leading to more successful outcomes.

Creativity is also a valuable skill when it comes to problem-solving. Thinking outside the box and considering innovative solutions can lead to breakthroughs that may not have been immediately apparent. Creativity allows individuals to explore different perspectives and come up with unique approaches to solving problems. By fostering creativity, individuals can open up new possibilities and generate fresh ideas to tackle even the most complex challenges.

Effective communication is another important aspect of problem-solving. Being able to clearly articulate ideas, share information, and collaborate with others is crucial in finding solutions to problems. Communicating effectively can help individuals gather input from others, seek advice, and work together to find the best possible solution. By fostering strong communication skills, individuals can build relationships, foster teamwork, and ultimately achieve greater success in problem-solving.

Adaptability is also key when it comes to problem-solving. The ability to adjust strategies, pivot quickly, and remain flexible in the face of challenges is crucial for overcoming unforeseen obstacles. Being adaptable allows individuals to respond to changes in circumstances, adjust their approach as needed, and continue moving forward towards a solution. By developing adaptability, individuals can better navigate uncertain situations and find solutions in even the most challenging environments. By developing strong problem-solving skills, individuals can identify issues, analyze them effectively, and come up with innovative solutions. Through critical thinking, creativity, effective communication, and adaptability, individuals can overcome obstacles, make informed decisions, and achieve their goals. By cultivating these skills, individuals can build confidence, resilience, and success in problem-solving.

- Developing Critical Thinking and Judgment

Critical thinking and judgment are two essential skills that are crucial for success in both academic and professional settings. These skills allow individuals to analyze information, evaluate arguments, and make informed decisions. Developing critical thinking and judgment takes time and practice, but the benefits are well worth the effort. In this essay, we will explore the importance of critical thinking and judgment, as well as some strategies for developing these skills.

Critical thinking is the ability to think clearly and rationally, understanding the logical connection between ideas. It involves being able to analyze and evaluate information, and to draw s based on evidence rather than emotion or personal bias. Critical thinking is an essential skill for success in all areas of life, as it allows individuals to make reasoned decisions, solve problems, and communicate effectively.

Judgment, on the other hand, is the ability to make decisions and form opinions based on careful consideration and evaluation of all available information. Judgment involves weighing the evidence, considering different perspectives, and making a informed decision. Good judgment is essential for success in both personal and professional life, as it allows individuals to make sound decisions that are based on reason rather than emotion.

Developing critical thinking and judgment requires practice and effort. One of the best ways to improve these skills is to actively engage with information and ideas, rather than passively accepting them. This involves asking questions, seeking out different perspectives, and evaluating evidence. It also involves being willing to change your mind in the face of new information, and being open to feedback and constructive criticism.

Another important aspect of developing critical thinking and judgment is being able to distinguish between fact and opinion. This involves being able to separate out objective information from subjective beliefs or feelings. Being able to recognize the difference between fact and opinion is crucial for making informed decisions and forming sound judgments.

One strategy for improving critical thinking and judgment is to practice active listening. By actively listening to others and considering their perspectives, individuals can gain a deeper understanding of different viewpoints and learn to think more critically about issues. Active listening involves asking questions, seeking clarification, and reflecting on what others have said before responding.

Another strategy for developing critical thinking and judgment is to engage in debate and discussion. By engaging in dialogue with others who hold different opinions, individuals can sharpen their critical thinking skills and learn to evaluate arguments from multiple perspectives. Debate and discussion can also help individuals practice forming and defending their own opinions, which is an essential aspect of good judgment.

In addition to practicing active listening and engaging in debate and discussion, individuals can also improve their critical thinking and judgment skills by developing a habit of skepticism. By questioning assumptions, seeking out evidence, and considering different possibilities, individuals can learn to think more critically and make better judgments.

To draw to a close, developing critical thinking and judgment also involves being willing to admit when you are wrong and being open to new ideas. By being willing to reconsider your beliefs in light of new evidence, you can avoid falling into the trap of confirmation bias and make more informed decisions. By actively engaging with information, distinguishing between fact and opinion, practicing active listening, engaging in debate and discussion, developing a habit of skepticism, and being open to new ideas, individuals can improve their critical thinking and judgment skills. These skills are not only important for academic and professional success, but also for personal growth and development. By investing time and effort in developing critical thinking and judgment, individuals can become more effective decision-makers and communicators, and lead more fulfilling and successful lives.

••••

- CONFLICT RESOLUTION Skills

Conflict resolution skills are essential in both personal and professional settings. When individuals are able to effectively address and resolve conflicts, it can lead to increased productivity, better relationships, and an overall more positive work environment. Conflict is a natural part of human interactions, as individuals have different perspectives, values, and opinions. However, how conflicts are managed and resolved can greatly impact the outcome and the relationships involved.

There are several key skills that are important for effective conflict resolution. One of the most important skills is communication. Being able to express oneself clearly and listen actively to others can help prevent misunderstandings and defuse tense situations. Active listening involves paying attention to what the other person is saying without interrupting, asking clarifying questions, and reflecting back what was said to ensure understanding.

Another important skill for conflict resolution is empathy. Empathy involves being able to put oneself in another person's shoes and understand their perspective and feelings. By demonstrating empathy, individuals can show that they care about the other person's feelings and are willing to work towards a mutually beneficial solution. This can help build trust and rapport, which is important for resolving conflicts effectively.

Problem-solving skills are also important for conflict resolution. Being able to identify the root cause of the conflict, brainstorm potential solutions, and evaluate the pros and cons of each solution can help individuals find a resolution that is fair and satisfactory for all parties involved. It is important to approach conflict resolution with a collaborative mindset, focusing on finding win-win solutions rather than trying to "win" the argument.

Managing emotions is another important skill for conflict resolution. Emotions can often escalate conflicts and make it difficult to approach the situation rationally. By being aware of one's own emotions and finding healthy ways to manage them, individuals can approach conflict resolution in a calm and constructive manner. It is also important to recognize when emotions are getting out of control and take a break if needed to cool off before continuing the discussion.

Lastly, it is important to be able to negotiate and compromise during conflict resolution. Compromise involves finding a middle ground that both parties can agree on, while negotiation involves finding creative solutions that address the needs and interests of both parties. By being open to compromise and negotiation, individuals can find solutions that are mutually beneficial and maintain positive relationships with others. By developing effective communication, empathy, problem-solving, emotion management, and negotiation skills, individuals can address conflicts in a constructive and collaborative manner. Conflict resolution skills are not only important for resolving conflicts that arise, but also for preventing conflicts from escalating and building stronger relationships with others. By practicing and honing these skills, individuals can create a more harmonious and productive environment both personally and professionally.

- Dealing with Anger and Frustration

Dealing with anger and frustration is a common challenge that many individuals face in their daily lives. Whether it's due to work stress, relationship issues, or other personal struggles, these negative emotions can take a toll on our mental and physical well-being if not addressed effectively. In this discussion, we will explore some strategies and techniques for managing anger and frustration in a healthy and constructive manner.

One of the first steps in dealing with anger and frustration is to recognize and acknowledge these emotions when they arise. It is important to be aware of our feelings and their triggers, so that we can better understand where they are coming from and how to address them. This self-awareness can help us to respond to these emotions in a more controlled and rational manner, rather than reacting impulsively or explosively.

Once we have identified our anger and frustration, it is important to take a step back and give ourselves some space to cool down. This could involve taking a few deep breaths, going for a walk, or engaging in a calming activity such as meditation or yoga. By giving ourselves a break from the situation that is causing us distress, we can gain some perspective and think more clearly about how to address the issue.

Another helpful strategy for dealing with anger and frustration is to practice active listening and effective communication. Often, these negative emotions can stem from misunderstandings, miscommunication, or unmet expectations in our interactions with others. By listening attentively to the perspectives of others and expressing our own thoughts and feelings in a clear and respectful manner, we can often resolve conflicts and reduce tension before they escalate into anger and frustration.

In addition to improving our communication skills, it can be helpful to learn and practice techniques for managing stress and maintaining a positive mindset. This could involve engaging in regular physical exercise, setting aside time for relaxation and self-care, or practicing mindfulness and cognitive-behavioral techniques to reframe negative thoughts and emotions. By taking care of our physical and mental well-being, we can build resilience and coping strategies to better handle the challenges and pressures that can lead to anger and frustration.

It is also important to seek support from friends, family, or mental health professionals when dealing with persistent or overwhelming anger and frustration. Talking to a trusted confidant or seeking therapy can provide a safe and supportive space to explore and address the underlying causes of these emotions, as well as develop strategies for coping and managing them more effectively. By reaching out for help when needed, we can build a strong support network and find ways to work through our anger and frustration in a constructive and healthy manner. By recognizing, addressing, and managing these negative emotions in a constructive and healthy manner, we can improve our mental and physical well-being, strengthen our relationships, and build resilience in the face of life's challenges. With practice and perseverance, we can learn to navigate our emotions with greater ease and find greater peace and fulfillment in our lives.

- Building Emotional Regulation

Emotional regulation is a fundamental aspect of mental health and well-being that is essential for navigating the complexities of daily life. It encompasses the ability to manage and respond to emotions in a healthy and adaptive manner, allowing individuals to effectively cope with stress, maintain relationships, and make sound decisions. Building emotional regulation involves developing skills and strategies to identify, understand, and regulate one's emotions in a constructive way.

One key component of building emotional regulation is self-awareness. This involves the ability to recognize and label one's own emotions, as well as to understand the underlying reasons for those emotions. By increasing self-awareness, individuals can gain insight into their emotional triggers and patterns, allowing them to respond more effectively to challenging situations. Strategies for enhancing self-awareness may include mindfulness practices, journaling, or engaging in therapy to explore and process emotions in a safe and supportive environment.

Another important aspect of building emotional regulation is developing emotional intelligence. Emotional intelligence refers to the ability to recognize and understand both one's own emotions and the emotions of others, as well as to use this information to guide thoughts, behaviors, and interactions. By honing emotional intelligence skills, individuals can improve their capacity for empathy, communication, and conflict resolution. This can lead to stronger relationships, increased resilience, and enhanced overall well-being. Techniques for building emotional intelligence may include practicing active listening, seeking feedback from others, and engaging in role-playing exercises to improve interpersonal skills.

In addition to self-awareness and emotional intelligence, building emotional regulation also involves developing coping strategies for managing difficult emotions. This may include learning how to identify and challenge negative thought patterns, practicing relaxation techniques to reduce stress and anxiety, or engaging in activities that promote emotional well-being such as exercise, art, or spending time in nature. By cultivating a toolbox of coping strategies, individuals can better cope with emotional challenges and maintain a sense of balance and resilience.

Furthermore, building emotional regulation is a lifelong process that requires ongoing practice and self-reflection. It is important to recognize that emotions are a natural and essential part of the human experience, and that it is normal to experience a range of emotions, both positive and negative. By building emotional regulation skills, individuals can learn to navigate their emotions in a way that promotes mental health and well-being, allowing them to lead more fulfilling and satisfying lives. Through dedication and perseverance, individuals can cultivate emotional resilience and create a strong foundation for psychological growth and development. By honing these skills, individuals can navigate the complexities of daily life with greater ease, resilience, and emotional well-being. Through ongoing practice and self-reflection, individuals can cultivate emotional regulation skills that enhance their ability to cope with stress, maintain relationships, and make sound decisions. Ultimately, building emotional regulation is an essential component of mental health and well-being that can lead to a more fulfilling and satisfying life.

Chapter 12: Peer Influence and Group Dynamics

. . . .

- UNDERSTANDING GROUP Behavior

Groups are a fundamental part of human society, and understanding how individuals behave within group settings is crucial for effective teamwork, decision-making, and leadership. In this essay, we will explore the key concepts and theories of group behavior, including the formation of groups, group dynamics, group cohesion, roles within groups, and how groups make decisions. By gaining a deeper understanding of these concepts, we can better navigate and leverage group dynamics in various contexts, whether it be in the workplace, social settings, or other group environments.

Formation of Groups

Groups can be formed in a variety of ways, including through formal organizations, spontaneous gatherings, or social networks. The formation of a group is often influenced by factors such as shared goals, interests, values, or demographics. In many cases, individuals may self-select into groups based on similarities or common interests, while in other instances, groups may be formed through external forces such as work assignments or social obligations.

Once a group is formed, it typically goes through stages of development, starting with the initial formation stage and progressing through stages of storming, norming, performing, and adjourning. During the storming stage, conflicts may arise as group members establish their roles, norms, and expectations. The norming stage is characterized by increased cohesion and acceptance of group norms, leading to improved collaboration and productivity. In the performing stage, the group is able to work together effectively towards common goals, while the adjourning stage marks the end of the group's task or project.

Group Dynamics

Group dynamics refer to the patterns of interaction and behavior that occur within a group. These dynamics are influenced by a variety of factors, including the size of the group, the composition of the group, the level of cohesion among members, and the leadership style within the group. Understanding group dynamics is essential for managing conflicts, promoting collaboration, and maximizing the effectiveness of group performance.

One key concept in group dynamics is social identity theory, which posits that individuals derive a sense of identity and self-esteem from their group memberships. This theory helps explain why individuals may exhibit in-group bias, favoring members of their own group over outsiders, and why individuals may conform to group norms and expectations. In addition, group polarization is another important phenomenon in group dynamics, whereby groups tend to make more extreme decisions and take more risks than individuals would on their own.

Group Cohesion

Group cohesion refers to the degree of mutual attraction and camaraderie among group members. Cohesive groups are more likely to work together harmoniously, communicate effectively, and support one another in achieving common goals. Factors that contribute to group cohesion include shared goals, values, and experiences, as well as interpersonal relationships and emotional bonds among group members.

Research suggests that high levels of group cohesion are associated with increased group satisfaction, motivation, and performance. However, excessive cohesion can also lead to groupthink, a phenomenon in which group members prioritize harmony and consensus over critical thinking and independent decision-making. To mitigate the negative effects of groupthink, leaders can encourage diverse perspectives, promote open communication, and foster a culture of constructive dissent within the group.

Roles within Groups

Roles within groups refer to the specific functions, responsibilities, and behaviors that individuals adopt in order to contribute to the group's overall success. Roles can be formal or informal, based on job titles or assigned tasks, or emergent through interactions and collaborations within the group. In many groups, individuals may take on multiple roles or switch roles depending on the situation or task at hand.

Effective role allocation and coordination are essential for group performance and productivity. Belbin's Team Role Theory identifies nine key roles within groups, such as the coordinator, shaper, implementer, and team worker, each contributing unique skills and strengths to the group's success. By understanding and leveraging these roles, group members can better utilize their talents, delegate responsibilities effectively, and ensure that all tasks are completed in a timely and efficient manner.

Decision-making in Groups

Decision-making is a critical aspect of group behavior, as groups are often required to make complex choices, solve problems, and reach consensus on important issues. Group decision-making can vary in terms of the level of participation, influence, and satisfaction among group members. Different decision-making processes, such as consensus, democratic, autocratic, or consultative, can lead to different outcomes and levels of satisfaction within the group.

One important model of group decision-making is Tuckman's Model of Group Development, which identifies four stages in the decision-making process: forming, storming, norming, and performing. During the forming stage, group members gather information, identify goals, and establish ground rules for decision-making. In the storming stage, conflicts may arise as members express different perspectives and opinions. The norming stage involves reaching consensus, resolving conflicts, and making decisions, while the performing stage involves implementing decisions and evaluating outcomes. By understanding the key concepts and theories of group behavior, such as the formation of groups, group dynamics, group cohesion, roles within groups, and decision-making processes, we can better navigate and leverage group dynamics for improved collaboration, communication, and performance. Whether in the workplace, social settings, or other group environments, a deeper understanding of group behavior can enhance our ability to work effectively with others and achieve common goals. By fostering a culture of inclusivity, diversity, and open communication within groups, we can create more productive and fulfilling group experiences for all members.

- Positive Peer Groups and Community Support

The influence of peers and community members can have a significant impact on an individual's beliefs, attitudes, and actions. Positive peer groups provide support, encouragement, and a sense of belonging, which can help individuals develop healthy relationships and make positive choices. Additionally, community support offers resources, services, and opportunities for personal growth and development.

Peer groups are social networks of individuals who share similar interests, values, and experiences. These groups can be formal, such as a sports team or club, or informal, such as a group of friends who regularly spend time together. Positive peer groups foster a sense of camaraderie and mutual respect among members. They provide a safe and supportive environment where individuals can express themselves freely, seek advice and guidance, and receive feedback from their peers.

Community support refers to the resources, services, and activities available within a specific geographical area or online community. These resources can include social services, educational programs, recreational facilities, and volunteer opportunities. By offering access to various resources and services, communities empower individuals to address their needs and achieve their goals.

Positive peer groups and community support go hand in hand in promoting positive behavior and well-being. Peer groups can serve as a support system within a larger community, offering emotional support, encouragement, and a sense of belonging. In turn, community support can provide peer groups with access to additional resources, services, and opportunities for personal growth and development. By working together, peers and community members can create a supportive environment that fosters positive relationships, personal growth, and community engagement.

One of the key benefits of positive peer groups and community support is the sense of belonging and social connectedness they provide. Belonging to a supportive peer group can help individuals feel accepted, valued, and understood. Likewise, being part of a community that offers support and resources can create a sense of connection and belonging.

Furthermore, positive peer groups and community support can help individuals develop a sense of identity and self-esteem. By interacting with peers who share similar values and interests, individuals can explore different aspects of themselves, gain self-awareness, and build self-confidence. Likewise, receiving support and encouragement from community members can boost self-esteem and motivate individuals to pursue their goals and aspirations. This positive reinforcement can help individuals overcome challenges, take risks, and achieve personal growth.

In addition to promoting social connectedness and self-esteem, positive peer groups and community support can also foster healthy relationships and positive communication skills. Within a positive peer group, individuals learn how to build trust, respect, and empathy with others. They practice conflict resolution, active listening, and effective communication skills, which are essential for building strong and healthy relationships. Similarly, community support offers opportunities for individuals to interact with a diverse group of people, develop social skills, and learn how to collaborate and cooperate with others towards a common goal.

Moreover, positive peer groups and community support can provide a sense of purpose and motivation for individuals. By participating in activities, programs, and events organized by peer groups and community organizations, individuals can find meaning, fulfillment, and joy in their lives. This sense of purpose can inspire individuals to set goals, work towards their aspirations, and make positive contributions to their communities. Additionally, receiving support and encouragement from peers and community members can motivate individuals to overcome obstacles, persevere through challenges, and achieve success. By creating a supportive environment that fosters social connectedness, self-esteem, healthy relationships, and a sense of purpose, peer groups and community organizations play a crucial role in empowering individuals to reach their full potential and contribute to the well-being of their communities. Through collaboration, cooperation, and mutual support, peers and community members can create a positive and inclusive environment where everyone can thrive and succeed.

- Addressing Negative Peer Pressure

Negative peer pressure is a common phenomenon that many individuals face at some point in their lives, especially during adolescence. Peer pressure refers to the influence that peers can have on an individual's thoughts, behaviors, and actions. While peer pressure can be positive and encourage individuals to engage in healthy behaviors or try new experiences, it can also be negative and lead individuals to engage in risky or harmful behaviors.

Addressing negative peer pressure is essential for individuals to maintain their autonomy and make decisions that align with their values and goals.

One of the first steps in addressing negative peer pressure is to understand why individuals may feel pressured to conform to the behaviors or expectations of their peers. Research has shown that adolescents are particularly susceptible to peer pressure due to their heightened sensitivity to social acceptance and desire to fit in with their peers. This desire for social acceptance can lead individuals to engage in behaviors that they may not necessarily agree with or feel comfortable doing. It is important for individuals to recognize that they have the power to make their own choices and that they do not have to conform to the expectations of others.

Another important aspect of addressing negative peer pressure is building strong self-esteem and self-confidence. Individuals who have a strong sense of self and are confident in their own abilities are less likely to succumb to negative peer pressure. Building self-esteem can involve engaging in activities that build confidence, setting and achieving personal goals, and surrounding oneself with supportive and positive influences. By developing a strong sense of self-worth, individuals are better equipped to resist negative peer pressure and make decisions that are in alignment with their values.

Communication is key when it comes to addressing negative peer pressure. Individuals should feel comfortable expressing their thoughts, feelings, and boundaries to their peers. This may involve setting clear boundaries and saying no to behaviors that go against one's values or beliefs. Effective communication can help individuals assert themselves and stand up to negative peer pressure in a respectful and assertive manner. It is important for individuals to remember that it is okay to say no and that they have the right to make their own choices.

Seeking support from trusted adults, such as parents, teachers, or counselors, can also be helpful in addressing negative peer pressure. These individuals can provide guidance, advice, and a listening ear to help individuals navigate challenging social situations. Trusted adults can also help individuals develop coping strategies for dealing with negative peer pressure and provide a supportive environment where individuals can express their concerns and seek guidance. Having a strong support system in place can make it easier for individuals to resist negative peer pressure and make decisions that are in their best interest. By understanding the reasons behind negative peer pressure, building self-esteem and self-confidence, communicating effectively, and seeking support from trusted adults, individuals can resist negative peer pressure and make choices that are in their best interest. It is important for individuals to remember that they have the power to make their own decisions and that they do not have to conform to the expectations of others. By taking proactive steps to address negative peer pressure, individuals can build resilience, assert themselves, and cultivate positive relationships with their peers.

Chapter 13: Building Resilience and Coping Skills

....

- TEACHING TEENS TO Bounce Back from Setbacks

Teaching teenagers how to bounce back from setbacks is an essential skill that can benefit them throughout their lives. Adolescence is a time of great change and growth, and teenagers are faced with a myriad of challenges that can sometimes feel overwhelming. Whether it's a disappointing grade on a test, a rejection from a college or job application, or a disagreement with a friend, setbacks are an inevitable part of life. Learning how to cope with setbacks effectively can help teenagers build resilience, develop problem-solving skills, and ultimately thrive in the face of adversity.

One of the key aspects of teaching teens to bounce back from setbacks is to help them understand that setbacks are a natural and normal part of life. It's important for teenagers to realize that everyone experiences setbacks at some point, and that it's not a reflection of their worth or abilities. By normalizing setbacks and framing them as opportunities for growth and learning, teenagers can begin to develop a healthier perspective on failure and setbacks. Encouraging teenagers to reframe setbacks as learning experiences can help them cultivate a growth mindset, which is essential for resilience and self-improvement.

In addition to reframing setbacks, it's important to help teenagers develop healthy coping mechanisms for dealing with setbacks when they do occur. Encouraging teenagers to practice self-care, such as engaging in activities they enjoy, getting enough sleep, and eating well, can help them cope with the stress and disappointment that often accompany setbacks. Teaching teenagers mindfulness techniques, such as deep breathing or meditation, can also help them regulate their emotions and stay grounded in the face of setbacks. By teaching teenagers healthy coping mechanisms early on, we can help them develop the skills they need to navigate the challenges of adolescence and beyond.

Another important aspect of teaching teenagers to bounce back from setbacks is to help them develop problem-solving skills. Encouraging teenagers to approach setbacks as challenges to be overcome can help them develop a proactive mindset and a sense of agency in the face of adversity. By helping teenagers break down setbacks into manageable steps, identify potential solutions, and take action to address them, we can empower them to become more resilient and self-reliant. By teaching teenagers how to problem-solve effectively, we can help them build confidence in their ability to overcome obstacles and setbacks.

To recapitulate, it's important to foster a supportive and encouraging environment for teenagers as they navigate setbacks. Providing teenagers with a strong support system of friends, family, teachers, and mentors can help them feel validated, understood, and cared for during challenging times. Encouraging teenagers to seek help and support when they need it, whether it's talking to a counselor, reaching out to a trusted adult, or confiding in a friend, can help them feel less alone and more resilient in the face of setbacks. By fostering a supportive environment for teenagers, we can help them build the social and emotional skills they need to bounce back from setbacks and thrive in the face of adversity. By helping teenagers develop a healthy perspective on setbacks, cultivate coping mechanisms, develop problem-solving skills, and foster a supportive environment, we can empower them to build resilience, self-confidence, and agency in the face of adversity. By equipping teenagers with the tools they need to bounce back from setbacks, we can help them develop the skills they need to thrive in an ever-changing and unpredictable world.

- Developing Coping Strategies for Stressful Situations

Stress is a common and natural response to challenging situations, demanding tasks, and overwhelming circumstances. While it is normal to experience stress from time to time, chronic stress can have detrimental effects on both our physical and mental health. In order to effectively manage and cope with stressful situations, it is important to develop coping strategies that help us navigate through difficult times with resilience and grace.

One of the key components of developing coping strategies for stressful situations is self-awareness. It is essential to recognize and acknowledge when we are feeling stressed, as this awareness allows us to take proactive steps to address the root cause of our stress. By identifying the triggers of our stress, we can better understand how to cope with it in a healthy and productive manner. This self-awareness also enables us to recognize when we need to seek support from others, whether that be through talking to a friend, reaching out to a therapist, or practicing self-care activities.

Another important aspect of coping with stressful situations is building a strong support network. Connecting with others who can provide emotional support, guidance, and encouragement during difficult times can greatly enhance our ability to cope with stress. Having a supportive network of family, friends, colleagues, or mental health professionals can offer different perspectives and insights that can help us navigate through challenging situations with more ease. In addition, sharing our feelings and experiences with others can help us feel less isolated and more understood, which can improve our overall sense of well-being.

In addition to seeking support from others, it is also important to take care of ourselves physically, emotionally, and mentally when facing stressful situations. Engaging in activities that promote relaxation and stress relief, such as exercise, meditation, deep breathing, or creative expression, can help us manage our stress levels and improve our overall resilience. Taking breaks when needed, setting boundaries, and practicing self-compassion are also crucial in maintaining our well-being during stressful times. By prioritizing self-care and making time for activities that bring us joy and relaxation, we can better cope with stress and build our resilience for future challenges.

Furthermore, developing effective coping strategies for stressful situations involves cultivating a positive mindset and attitude. Instead of focusing on the negative aspects of a stressful situation, try to reframe your thoughts in a more positive light. For example, instead of viewing a challenging task as overwhelming and impossible to complete, try to see it as an opportunity for growth, learning, and personal development. By shifting your perspective and focusing on the potential benefits or lessons that can be gained from a stressful situation, you can approach challenges with a sense of optimism, resilience, and determination. By cultivating self-awareness, building a strong support network, practicing self-care, and maintaining a positive mindset, we can better manage our stress levels and navigate through challenging times with grace and resilience. Remember that it is okay to seek help when needed and to prioritize your well-being during stressful situations. By taking proactive steps to cope with stress, you can build your resilience and empower yourself to face future challenges with confidence and strength.

- Building Resilience through Challenges

Building resilience is a crucial aspect of personal growth and development. In today's fast-paced and constantly changing world, individuals are faced with numerous challenges and obstacles that can test their ability to cope and adapt. Resilience is the ability to bounce back from setbacks, to persevere in the face of adversity, and to remain positive and focused in the midst of challenges. It is a skill that can be learned and developed over time, and it is essential for achieving success in both personal and professional endeavors.

One of the key ways to build resilience is through facing and overcoming challenges. Challenges are a normal part of life, and they can come in many different forms – from minor setbacks and disappointments to major crises and upheavals. When we are faced with challenges, it is natural to feel stressed, anxious, and overwhelmed. However, by approaching challenges with a positive attitude and a growth mindset, we can turn them into opportunities for learning and growth.

When we face challenges, we are forced to step outside of our comfort zone and confront our fears and limitations. This can be uncomfortable and even painful at times, but it is through facing and overcoming challenges that we build resilience and develop the strength and confidence to handle whatever life throws our way. Challenges can provide valuable lessons and insights that help us to grow and evolve as individuals, and they can also serve as a catalyst for personal and professional development.

In order to build resilience through challenges, it is important to cultivate a positive mindset and to develop a sense of self-efficacy. Self-efficacy is the belief in one's own ability to succeed and to overcome obstacles. When we have a strong sense of self-efficacy, we are more likely to approach challenges with confidence and determination, and we are better equipped to persevere in the face of setbacks. By building our self-efficacy through small wins and successes, we can gradually increase our resilience and develop the inner strength and resilience needed to face bigger challenges.

Another important aspect of building resilience through challenges is to cultivate a growth mindset. A growth mindset is the belief that our abilities and intelligence are not fixed, but can be developed through effort and perseverance. When we approach challenges with a growth mindset, we are more likely to see them as opportunities for learning and growth, rather than as threats to our well-being. By embracing challenges as a way to stretch and expand our capabilities, we can build resilience and become more adaptive and flexible in the face of change.

In addition to developing a positive mindset and a growth mindset, it is important to cultivate self-care practices that can help us to manage stress and build resilience. Self-care practices can include things like regular exercise, healthy eating, adequate sleep, mindfulness meditation, and relaxation techniques. By taking care of our physical, emotional, and mental well-being, we can strengthen our resilience and increase our ability to cope with challenges.

In brief, building resilience through challenges also involves seeking support from others. It is important to cultivate strong social connections and to reach out for help when needed. By sharing our struggles and seeking support from friends, family, colleagues, or mental health professionals, we can gain new perspectives, insights, and resources that can help us to navigate challenges and build resilience. Building a strong support network can provide us with the encouragement, reassurance, and guidance that we need to weather storms and emerge stronger and more resilient on the other side. By cultivating a positive mindset, a growth mindset, self-efficacy, self-care practices, and social support, we can strengthen our resilience and increase our ability to cope with the ups and downs of life. Challenges can be daunting, but they can also be powerful catalysts for personal growth and development. By embracing challenges as opportunities for learning and growth, we can build resilience and become more resilient, adaptive, and resilient individuals.

Chapter 14: Time Management and Organization

· · · ·

- BALANCING RESPONSIBILITIES and Prioritizing Tasks

Balancing responsibilities and prioritizing tasks is a fundamental skill that is crucial for success in both personal and professional endeavors. In today's fast-paced and constantly evolving world, individuals are often faced with a multitude of responsibilities and tasks that demand their attention and time. Whether it be managing a busy work schedule, taking care of personal commitments, or pursuing academic goals, the ability to effectively balance responsibilities and prioritize tasks is essential for achieving desired outcomes and maintaining a sense of control and well-being.

The first step in achieving a balance between responsibilities and tasks is to clearly define and identify them. It is important to take stock of all the responsibilities and tasks that need to be addressed, whether they are work-related, personal, or academic. By creating a comprehensive list, individuals can gain a better understanding of the scope of their obligations and can begin to prioritize them based on their level of importance and urgency.

Once all responsibilities and tasks have been identified, the next step is to prioritize them based on their importance and deadline. Prioritization allows individuals to focus their time and energy on the most critical tasks and ensures that they are completed in a timely manner. One helpful tool for prioritizing tasks is the Eisenhower Matrix, which categorizes tasks into four quadrants based on their importance and urgency. By using this framework, individuals can easily identify which tasks require immediate attention and which can be postponed or delegated.

In addition to prioritizing tasks based on importance and urgency, it is also essential to consider other factors such as resources, skill level, and capacity. It is important to be realistic about what can be achieved within a given timeframe and to allocate resources accordingly. This may involve delegating tasks to others, seeking help or support from colleagues or friends, or re-evaluating time management strategies to ensure that tasks are completed efficiently and effectively.

Another key aspect of balancing responsibilities and prioritizing tasks is the ability to adapt and be flexible in the face of changing circumstances. In today's constantly evolving world, unexpected challenges and issues are bound to arise, throwing even the most carefully planned schedules off track. It is important to be prepared for such eventualities and to be able to adjust priorities and tasks accordingly. This may involve reevaluating deadlines, reassessing the importance of tasks, or reallocating resources to address new challenges and opportunities.

In order to maintain a healthy balance between responsibilities and tasks, it is also important to take care of oneself and prioritize self-care. This includes setting aside time for rest and relaxation, engaging in activities that bring joy and fulfillment, and maintaining a healthy work-life balance. By prioritizing self-care, individuals can recharge their energy levels, reduce stress and burnout, and improve overall well-being, which in turn can lead to increased productivity and effectiveness in managing responsibilities and tasks. By clearly defining and identifying responsibilities, prioritizing tasks based on importance and urgency, considering resources and capacity, adapting to changing circumstances, and prioritizing self-care, individuals can maintain a sense of control and balance in their lives and achieve success in both personal and professional endeavors.

- Developing Time Management Skills

Time management is a crucial skill that is essential for success in both personal and professional life. It involves the ability to prioritize tasks, set goals, and allocate time effectively to ensure that all responsibilities are completed in a timely manner. Developing effective time management skills can have a significant impact on productivity, efficiency, and overall well-being. In this article, we will explore the importance of time management, as well as practical strategies for improving this skill.

One of the key benefits of developing strong time management skills is increased productivity. When you are able to prioritize tasks and allocate time effectively, you can accomplish more in less time. This can lead to a greater sense of accomplishment and satisfaction, as well as increased confidence in your ability to handle multiple responsibilities. By staying organized and focused on your goals, you can avoid wasting time on unimportant tasks and ensure that you are making the most of your time.

In addition to increased productivity, effective time management can also help reduce stress and anxiety. When you have a clear plan for how you will spend your time and are able to stay on track with your tasks, you are less likely to feel overwhelmed or rushed. This can lead to a greater sense of calm and control, as well as improved overall well-being. By managing your time effectively, you can create a healthy work-life balance and avoid burnout.

Developing strong time management skills can also improve your ability to meet deadlines and achieve your goals. By setting clear priorities and timelines for each task, you can stay on track with your projects and ensure that you are able to complete them on time. This can lead to greater success in both your personal and professional life, as well as increased opportunities for advancement and recognition. By consistently meeting deadlines and achieving your goals, you can build a reputation as a reliable and effective individual who can be counted on to deliver results.

There are several practical strategies that can help you improve your time management skills. One of the most important steps is to prioritize your tasks and focus on those that are most important and urgent. By identifying your top priorities and allocating time to them first, you can ensure that you are spending your time on tasks that will have the greatest impact on your goals. This can help you avoid getting bogged down in unimportant or time-consuming tasks and ensure that you are making progress towards your objectives.

Another key strategy for effective time management is to break down larger tasks into smaller, more manageable steps. By breaking a larger project into smaller tasks and setting deadlines for each one, you can make the project more manageable and prevent feeling overwhelmed. This can help you stay focused and on track with your tasks, as well as ensure that you are able to make steady progress towards your goals. By breaking tasks down into smaller steps, you can also create a sense of accomplishment and motivation as you complete each one.

It is also important to set realistic goals and deadlines for yourself, taking into account your workload, personal commitments, and other responsibilities. By setting clear, achievable goals and deadlines, you can create a roadmap for how you will spend your time and ensure that you are able to make progress towards your objectives. This can help you stay on track with your tasks and avoid getting overwhelmed by unrealistic expectations. By setting goals and deadlines that are attainable, you can build a sense of momentum and motivation as you work towards achieving them.

Effective time management also involves the ability to eliminate distractions and stay focused on your tasks. In today's fast-paced world, it can be easy to get distracted by email, social media, and other interruptions that can derail your progress. By setting boundaries and creating a focused work environment, you can minimize distractions and stay on track with your tasks. This can help you maximize your productivity and ensure that you are making the most of your time. By eliminating distractions and staying focused, you can create a more productive and efficient work environment that allows you to accomplish more in less time. By prioritizing tasks, setting goals, and allocating time effectively, you can improve your productivity, reduce stress, and achieve your goals. By implementing practical strategies such as prioritizing tasks, breaking down larger projects into smaller steps, setting realistic goals and deadlines, and eliminating distractions, you can enhance your time management skills and maximize your efficiency. By consistently practicing these strategies and making time management a priority in your daily routine, you can create a more organized and focused approach to your tasks and achieve greater success in all areas of your life.

- Creating Healthy Routines and Schedules

Creating healthy routines and schedules is essential for maintaining a balanced and productive lifestyle. Developing consistent routines can help improve overall well-being and reduce stress levels. By establishing daily habits and setting a schedule, individuals can better manage their time, prioritize tasks, and maintain a sense of control over their daily lives. In this article, we will explore the benefits of creating healthy routines and schedules, as well as provide practical tips and strategies for implementing them effectively.

One of the key benefits of creating healthy routines and schedules is that they can help promote overall physical and mental health. By establishing regular sleep patterns, meal times, exercise routines, and relaxation periods, individuals can improve their quality of life and reduce the risk of health problems such as obesity, heart disease, and depression. Routines can also help individuals cope with stress more effectively by providing structure and predictability to their day-to-day lives. This can lead to improved focus, concentration, and decision-making abilities, as well as a greater sense of well-being and satisfaction.

Another benefit of creating healthy routines and schedules is that they can enhance productivity and efficiency. By setting specific goals, breaking tasks down into manageable steps, and allocating time for each activity, individuals can better prioritize their responsibilities and make the most of their time. This can lead to increased motivation, creativity, and overall performance in both personal and professional endeavors. Additionally, routines can help individuals stay on track with their goals and make progress towards achieving them, leading to a greater sense of accomplishment and fulfillment.

In order to create healthy routines and schedules, it is important to first identify your priorities and goals. This may include determining what tasks are most important to you, what activities bring you joy and fulfillment, and what areas of your life could benefit from more structure and organization. Once you have a clear understanding of your priorities, you can begin to establish a daily or weekly schedule that reflects these goals and incorporates activities that are important to you.

When creating a schedule, it is important to be realistic and flexible. It is important to leave room for unexpected events or changes in plans, and to be willing to adjust your schedule as needed. By being adaptable and open to new opportunities, you can ensure that your routines remain effective and sustainable over time. It is also important to set aside time for self-care and relaxation, as well as for social activities and relationships, in order to maintain a healthy work-life balance.

In addition to establishing a daily schedule, it can also be helpful to develop specific routines for certain activities or tasks. For example, you may want to create a morning routine that includes exercise, healthy breakfast, and meditation to start your day off on the right foot. Or you may want to establish a bedtime routine that includes relaxation techniques, such as reading or listening to music, to help you unwind and prepare for sleep. By creating these routines, you can establish healthy habits that can improve your overall well-being and make it easier to stay on track with your goals. By establishing consistent habits and setting a schedule, individuals can improve their physical and mental health, enhance their productivity and efficiency, and achieve a greater sense of well-being and satisfaction. By identifying your priorities and goals, being realistic and flexible, and developing specific routines for certain activities, you can create a schedule that works for you and helps you make the most of your time and energy. With practice and perseverance, you can establish healthy routines and schedules that support your overall well-being and lead to a more fulfilling and fulfilling life.

Chapter 15: Parenting Styles and Strategies

• • • •

- POSITIVE PARENTING Techniques

Positive parenting techniques are crucial for the healthy development and well-being of children. By utilizing positive and nurturing strategies, parents can foster a strong bond with their children, promote positive behavior, and create a supportive and loving environment in which their children can thrive. Positive parenting involves establishing clear expectations and boundaries, providing consistent and fair discipline, and offering praise and encouragement to reinforce desired behaviors. It also involves active listening, empathy, and effective communication to build strong relationships and understanding between parents and children.

One key aspect of positive parenting is the use of positive reinforcement to encourage and reinforce desired behaviors in children. This involves praising and rewarding children when they exhibit positive behaviors, such as helping out around the house, showing kindness to others, or demonstrating good manners. By acknowledging and celebrating these behaviors, parents can help their children feel valued and appreciated, which can boost their self-esteem and confidence. Positive reinforcement can also help children learn to associate positive actions with positive outcomes, making them more likely to repeat these behaviors in the future.

Another important component of positive parenting is setting clear expectations and boundaries for children. By establishing consistent rules and consequences, parents can help children understand what is expected of them and what will happen if they fail to meet these expectations. Clear boundaries also provide children with a sense of structure and security, which can help them feel safe and supported in their environment. Parents should communicate these expectations clearly and consistently, and be prepared to enforce consequences when necessary. However, it is also important for parents to be flexible and open to negotiation, as children may sometimes need help understanding and following rules.

Effective communication is key to positive parenting, as it helps parents understand their child's needs and feelings, and allows children to express themselves and be heard. Parents should strive to be good listeners, showing empathy and understanding when their children talk about their thoughts, feelings, and experiences. By actively listening to their children and validating their emotions, parents can build trust and strengthen their relationship with them. Communication should be respectful and nonjudgmental, and parents should strive to speak honestly and openly with their children, providing guidance and support while allowing them to express themselves freely.

Positive parenting also involves providing children with opportunities to learn and grow, both academically and emotionally. Parents can support their children's education by helping them with their homework, encouraging them to read and explore new topics, and advocating for their educational needs. They can also help their children develop social and emotional skills by teaching them how to resolve conflicts, manage their emotions, and build healthy relationships with others. By fostering a love of learning and providing guidance and support, parents can help their children develop the skills and confidence they need to succeed in school and in life. By using positive reinforcement, setting clear expectations and boundaries, practicing effective communication, and providing opportunities for learning and growth, parents can build strong and healthy relationships with their children, promote positive behavior, and instill values and beliefs that will guide them throughout their lives. Positive parenting is a lifelong journey that requires patience, understanding, and dedication, but the rewards of raising happy, healthy, and well-adjusted children are well worth the effort. By embracing positive parenting techniques, parents can create a positive and loving home environment that will benefit their children for years to come.

- Discipline vs. Punishment

Discipline and punishment are two terms often used interchangeably, but they actually have distinct meanings and purposes when it comes to behavior management. Discipline is a proactive approach that focuses on teaching and guiding individuals to make positive choices and learn from their mistakes. It is rooted in respect, consistency, and clear communication. Punishment, on the other hand, is a reactive response to negative behavior that is intended to inflict some form of pain or suffering as a deterrent. While both discipline and punishment are tools used to address inappropriate behavior, they have different effects on the individual being disciplined.

Discipline, when implemented effectively, fosters a sense of responsibility and accountability in individuals. It helps them develop self-control, empathy, and problem-solving skills that are essential for their personal and professional growth. Discipline is about setting clear expectations, providing structure and boundaries, and offering support and guidance to help individuals make better choices. It is about teaching individuals the skills they need to navigate challenges and conflicts in a constructive way. Discipline is not about control or coercion; rather, it is about empowerment and self-improvement.

In contrast, punishment can have negative consequences that may hinder the individual's development and relationship with authority figures. Punishment often creates feelings of resentment, hostility, and shame, which can impact an individual's self-esteem and self-worth. Punishment is more about control and compliance rather than teaching individuals how to behave appropriately. It focuses on consequences rather than on understanding the underlying reasons for the behavior. Punishment can also lead to a cycle of retaliation, where individuals respond to being punished by engaging in more negative behavior.

Discipline and punishment are also rooted in different philosophical beliefs about human behavior and motivation. Discipline is based on the belief that individuals are capable of learning and growing from their mistakes when provided with the necessary support and guidance. It recognizes that behavior is influenced by a variety of factors, including social, emotional, and cognitive processes. Discipline seeks to address the root causes of behavior and help individuals develop the skills they need to make positive choices. In contrast, punishment is based on the belief that fear and discomfort are effective motivators for changing behavior. It focuses on external consequences rather than on internal growth and development.

It is important to note that discipline and punishment are not mutually exclusive; they can be used together in a balanced and thoughtful manner. Discipline can involve consequences for negative behavior, but these consequences are intended to be educational and constructive rather than punitive. Discipline also involves positive reinforcement for desired behavior, such as praise, rewards, and privileges. Punishment, when used sparingly and in conjunction with discipline, can serve as a deterrent for more serious or dangerous behavior. However, punishment should never be the primary tool for managing behavior, as it can have long-lasting negative effects on individuals' emotional and psychological well-being. Discipline focuses on teaching, guiding, and empowering individuals to make positive choices and learn from their mistakes. Punishment, on the other hand, relies on fear and discomfort as motivators for changing behavior. While both discipline and punishment can be effective tools for addressing inappropriate behavior, it is important to use discipline as the primary approach and reserve punishment for serious or dangerous behavior. By understanding the differences between discipline and punishment and using them in a thoughtful and balanced manner, we can help individuals develop the skills they need to thrive in all aspects of their lives.

- Collaborative Parenting Approaches

Collaborative parenting approaches refer to a method of parenting where both parents work together to raise their children in a supportive and constructive manner. This approach emphasizes communication, teamwork, and mutual respect between parents as they navigate the challenges and joys of raising a family. Collaborative parenting recognizes that each parent brings their own unique strengths, perspectives, and experiences to the partnership, and that by combining these resources, they can create a more effective and harmonious parenting environment for their children.

One of the key tenets of collaborative parenting is open and honest communication between parents. This means that parents should actively listen to each other, express their thoughts and feelings clearly, and work together to find solutions to parenting challenges. By communicating openly and respectfully, parents can avoid misunderstandings and conflicts, and build a strong foundation of trust and partnership in their co-parenting relationship. Effective communication also involves setting aside time to discuss parenting strategies, goals, and concerns, and to make joint decisions about important issues affecting their children.

In addition to communication, collaboration parenting also involves shared decision-making and problem-solving. Parents should strive to make parenting decisions together, taking into account each other's viewpoints, priorities, and preferences. By involving both parents in the decision-making process, children can benefit from a more consistent and cohesive parenting approach that reflects both parents' values and beliefs. Collaborative problem-solving also means working together to address parenting challenges and conflicts in a constructive and respectful manner, rather than resorting to blame or criticism. By approaching problems as a team, parents can model positive conflict resolution skills for their children and create a more peaceful and harmonious home environment.

Another important aspect of collaborative parenting is mutual respect and support between parents. This means that parents should acknowledge and appreciate each other's contributions to the parenting partnership, and offer each other emotional support and encouragement when facing parenting challenges. By showing respect for each other's ideas, opinions, and decisions, parents can create a sense of equality and partnership in their co-parenting relationship. Mutual support also involves sharing the responsibilities of parenting, such as childcare, housework, and decision-making, in a fair and equitable manner. By working together as a team, parents can create a balanced and harmonious parenting environment that benefits both them and their children.

Collaborative parenting approaches also emphasize the importance of flexibility and adaptability in responding to the changing needs and dynamics of the family. Parents should be willing to adjust their parenting strategies, rules, and expectations as their children grow and develop, and as new challenges and opportunities arise. By remaining open to new ideas and perspectives, parents can continue to learn and grow as parents, and create a nurturing and supportive environment for their children. Flexibility also means being willing to compromise and negotiate with each other, in order to find solutions that meet the needs of both parents and children. By embracing change and adaptation, parents can create a more resilient and dynamic parenting partnership that can weather the ups and downs of family life. By emphasizing communication, teamwork, and mutual respect, parents can create a strong foundation of trust and partnership in their co-parenting relationship. Shared decision-making and problem-solving can help parents create a consistent and cohesive parenting approach that benefits their children.

Mutual support and respect can foster a sense of equality and cooperation in the parenting partnership. And flexibility and adaptability can help parents respond to the changing needs and dynamics of their family. By embracing collaborative parenting approaches, parents can create a nurturing and supportive environment for their children, and build a strong and healthy family unit that can thrive and grow together.

Chapter 16: Seeking Professional Help and Resources

. . . .

- ACCESSING MENTAL HEALTH Services

Accessing mental health services is a crucial step in maintaining and improving one's emotional well-being. As mental health awareness continues to grow, so does the availability of resources and support systems for those seeking help. However, navigating the complex landscape of mental health services can be overwhelming for many individuals. In this discussion, we will explore the various ways in which individuals can access mental health services, the different types of services available, and tips for finding the right provider for their needs.

One of the most common ways to access mental health services is through primary care physicians. Many individuals start by discussing their mental health concerns with their primary care provider, who can then refer them to a mental health specialist or counselor. This can be a convenient and efficient way to access services, as primary care providers often have existing relationships with mental health professionals and can provide valuable guidance and recommendations.

Another option for accessing mental health services is through community mental health centers. These centers offer a wide range of services, including individual counseling, group therapy, and psychiatric evaluations. Community mental health centers are often more affordable than private practices and can provide culturally sensitive care to individuals from diverse backgrounds.

For those who prefer a more personalized approach, private practice therapists and counselors are another option for accessing mental health services. Private practice providers offer individualized treatment plans tailored to the unique needs of each client. While private practice providers may be more expensive than other options, many individuals find that the personalized care and attention they receive are well worth the cost.

In addition to traditional therapy services, there are also a variety of online mental health resources available to individuals seeking support. Teletherapy, or therapy conducted via video chat or phone, has become increasingly popular in recent years. Online therapy platforms offer convenience and flexibility, allowing individuals to access care from the comfort of their own homes.

Peer support groups are another valuable resource for individuals seeking mental health services. Peer support groups bring together individuals who are facing similar challenges and provide a safe space for sharing experiences and strategies for coping. Peer support groups can be especially helpful for individuals who may feel isolated or alone in their struggles.

When seeking mental health services, it is important to consider factors such as accessibility, affordability, and cultural competence. Individuals should research and compare different providers to find the best fit for their needs. It may also be helpful to ask for recommendations from friends, family, or healthcare providers. With a growing awareness of mental health issues and an increasing availability of resources, individuals have more options than ever for seeking help. By exploring different types of services and providers, individuals can find the support they need to navigate their mental health challenges and lead happier, healthier lives.

- Finding Support Groups and Counseling

Support groups and counseling are vital resources for individuals facing a variety of challenges and difficulties in their lives. Whether one is dealing with mental health issues, grief and loss, addiction, or a chronic illness, these services offer a safe and supportive environment where individuals can share their experiences, receive guidance, and find emotional support. In this essay, we will explore the benefits of support groups and counseling, how to find the right group or therapist, and what to expect from these services.

Support groups are gatherings of individuals who share a common experience or struggle, such as living with a chronic illness, surviving a traumatic event, or going through a divorce. These groups provide a sense of community and belonging, as members can relate to each other's experiences and offer empathy and understanding. Support groups can be led by trained professionals or peers who have gone through similar challenges, and they typically meet on a regular basis to discuss their experiences, share coping strategies, and offer emotional support to one another.

Counseling, on the other hand, involves working one-on-one with a licensed therapist or counselor to address specific mental health concerns or life challenges. Counseling sessions can help individuals gain insight into their thoughts, feelings, and behaviors, and develop coping skills to manage stress, anxiety, depression, or other mental health issues. Therapists use a variety of techniques, such as talk therapy, cognitive-behavioral therapy, or mindfulness practices, to help their clients process their emotions and develop healthier ways of thinking and behaving.

Finding a support group or therapist that is the right fit for you can be a challenging process, but it is essential to take the time to research and explore your options. One way to find support groups in your area is to ask for recommendations from your healthcare provider, therapist, or local mental health organizations. Additionally, websites such as Meetup.com and Psychology Today offer directories of support groups and therapists in your area, along with user reviews and ratings to help you make an informed decision.

When looking for a therapist, it is important to consider their credentials, experience, and approach to therapy. Licensed therapists have completed extensive training and are held to ethical standards and regulations, ensuring that they provide quality care to their clients. It is also helpful to meet with a few therapists before making a decision, to see if you feel comfortable and supported in their presence. Trust and rapport are essential in the therapeutic relationship, so it is important to choose a therapist who you feel you can open up to and be honest with.

In addition to seeking professional help, there are also online resources and virtual support groups available for individuals who may not have access to in-person services. Online counseling platforms, such as BetterHelp and Talkspace, offer convenient and affordable therapy options for individuals who prefer to receive counseling from the comfort of their own home. Virtual support groups, forums, and social media communities also provide a space for individuals to connect with others who are going through similar challenges and receive support and encouragement.

Regardless of whether you choose to attend a support group, see a therapist, or engage in online counseling, it is important to remember that seeking help is a sign of strength, not weakness. Everyone goes through difficult times in their lives, and reaching out for support is a brave and empowering step towards healing and personal growth. Support groups and counseling can provide a safe and non-judgmental space for individuals to process their emotions, gain new perspectives, and develop coping strategies to navigate life's challenges. By taking the first step towards seeking help, you are investing in your well-being and creating a path towards a brighter and healthier future.

- Connecting with Community Resources

In today's complex and interconnected world, it is essential for individuals and organizations to tap into the various community resources available to them. These resources can range from local government agencies to nonprofit organizations, businesses, schools, and other community-based groups. By connecting with these resources, individuals can gain access to a wealth of knowledge, expertise, and support that can help them address a wide range of challenges and opportunities.

One of the key benefits of connecting with community resources is the ability to leverage the collective power of the community to address common challenges. For example, by working together with other organizations in the community, individuals can pool their resources, share best practices, and coordinate their efforts to achieve common goals. This collaborative approach can help amplify the impact of individual initiatives and lead to more sustainable and effective solutions.

In addition to the practical benefits of collaboration, connecting with community resources can also help individuals build relationships and networks that can be invaluable in both their personal and professional lives. By actively participating in community activities, individuals can meet and connect with a diverse range of people who may have valuable knowledge, skills, and connections that can help them achieve their goals. These relationships can also provide emotional support, encouragement, and motivation, helping individuals stay focused and committed to their objectives.

Furthermore, connecting with community resources can help individuals develop a deeper understanding of the community in which they live or work. By engaging with local organizations, attending community events, and participating in community initiatives, individuals can gain insights into the needs, challenges, and opportunities facing their community. This knowledge can help individuals better tailor their efforts to address the specific needs of the community and make a more meaningful impact.

When it comes to connecting with community resources, it is important for individuals to be proactive and strategic in their approach. This may involve conducting research to identify relevant resources, reaching out to key stakeholders to establish partnerships, and actively participating in community activities to build relationships and networks. It is also important for individuals to communicate openly and transparently with community members, sharing their goals, challenges, and achievements, and seeking feedback and input on their initiatives. By leveraging the expertise, resources, and networks available in the community, individuals can amplify their efforts, build valuable relationships, and gain insights into the needs and opportunities facing their community. Ultimately, by working together with others in the community, individuals can create a more vibrant, resilient, and inclusive community for all.

••••

- RECAP OF KEY POINTS

As we conclude our discussion on the key points covered throughout this topic, it is important to recap and reinforce the main ideas that have been presented. By summarizing the key takeaways, we can ensure that the information is clear and easily understood by all readers.

One of the primary themes that emerged from our discussion is the importance of effective communication in achieving success in both personal and professional endeavors. Communication skills are essential in building strong relationships, resolving conflicts, and fostering collaboration. By actively listening, asking clarifying questions, and expressing oneself clearly and confidently, individuals can enhance their communication abilities and navigate various situations with greater ease.

Another key point to highlight is the significance of setting and achieving goals. Goal setting provides direction, motivation, and a sense of purpose in our lives. By establishing clear, achievable, and measurable goals, individuals can track their progress, stay focused, and ultimately reach their desired outcomes. It is important to regularly review and adjust goals as needed to ensure they remain relevant and attainable.

Moreover, the importance of time management and prioritization cannot be overstated. Effectively managing one's time and tasks allows for increased productivity, reduced stress, and a greater sense of control over one's daily activities. By identifying priorities, breaking tasks into manageable steps, and allocating time and resources efficiently, individuals can optimize their performance and achieve their desired outcomes.

Additionally, the significance of resilience and adaptability in overcoming challenges and setbacks cannot be overlooked. Life is unpredictable, and unexpected obstacles will inevitably arise. Developing resilience, the ability to bounce back from adversity, and adaptability, the capacity to adjust to changing circumstances, are essential skills for navigating the ups and downs of life with grace and resilience.

Furthermore, self-awareness and emotional intelligence are critical components of personal and professional success. By understanding one's strengths, weaknesses, values, and emotions, individuals can make informed decisions, build strong relationships, and effectively navigate various social and emotional situations. Developing emotional intelligence through self-reflection, empathy, and active listening can enhance one's interpersonal skills and overall well-being. By incorporating these key principles into our daily lives and interactions, we can enhance our skills, relationships, and overall well-being. It is essential to continuously reflect on and apply these key points to our lives to drive growth, development, and fulfillment. Thank you for joining us on this journey of exploration and learning, and we look forward to further discussions and discoveries in the future.

- Continued Support and Guidance for Parents

Parenting is a complex and rewarding journey that requires continuous support and guidance. As children grow and develop, parents face new challenges and obstacles along the way. It is important for parents to have access to resources and tools that can help them navigate these challenges and ensure the well-being of their children. Continued support and guidance for parents can come in many forms, including educational workshops, online resources, and community programs. By providing parents with the resources they need, we can help them build a strong foundation for their children's future success.

One of the key aspects of continued support and guidance for parents is education. Parenting is a skill that requires knowledge and understanding of child development, behavior management, and effective communication. Educational workshops can provide parents with the information and tools they need to navigate the challenges of parenting. These workshops can cover a wide range of topics, including discipline strategies, positive parenting techniques, and effective communication skills. By attending these workshops, parents can gain valuable insights and practical tips that can help them become more confident and effective parents.

In addition to educational workshops, online resources can also be a valuable source of support and guidance for parents. The internet offers a wealth of information on parenting, from articles and blogs to videos and social media groups. Parents can access a wide range of resources at their fingertips, allowing them to learn from experts, connect with other parents, and find solutions to common parenting challenges. Online resources can be particularly helpful for parents who may not have access to in-person workshops or who prefer to learn at their own pace. By utilizing online resources, parents can stay informed and connected as they navigate the ups and downs of parenting.

Community programs can also play a crucial role in providing continued support and guidance for parents. These programs offer a wide range of services and resources, from parent support groups to childcare services to parenting classes. Community programs can provide parents with a sense of belonging and connection, allowing them to connect with other parents who may be facing similar challenges. By participating in these programs, parents can gain valuable support, advice, and resources that can help them navigate the complexities of parenting. Community programs can also provide parents with opportunities to engage in enriching activities with their children, strengthening the parent-child bond and promoting healthy development. By providing parents with educational workshops, online resources, and community programs, we can help them navigate the challenges of parenting and build a strong foundation for their children's future. It is important for parents to have access to the resources and tools they need to become confident and effective parents. By investing in the support and guidance of parents, we can create a positive and nurturing environment for children to thrive.

- Empowering Teens for Success

Empowering teens for success is a crucial aspect of preparing them for the future. As they navigate the complexities of adolescence and strive to find their place in the world, it is important to provide them with the tools and resources they need to thrive. By empowering teens, we are equipping them with the skills and confidence to overcome challenges, set goals, and reach their full potential. This not only benefits the individual teen but also society as a whole, as empowered teens are more likely to become successful, contributing members of their communities.

One of the key ways to empower teens for success is to provide them with a supportive and nurturing environment. This includes fostering positive relationships with parents, teachers, mentors, and peers who can offer guidance, encouragement, and support. When teens feel confident that they have a support system in place, they are more likely to take risks, set ambitious goals, and pursue their passions. Additionally, it is important to create a safe space for teens to express themselves, share their thoughts and feelings, and explore their interests. This can help them develop a strong sense of self-awareness and self-confidence, which are crucial for success in any endeavor.

Another important aspect of empowering teens for success is to help them develop essential life skills. This includes teaching them how to manage their time effectively, set and achieve goals, communicate effectively, and make responsible decisions. By providing teens with opportunities to practice these skills in real-world situations, we can help them build resilience, confidence, and a sense of agency. This can empower them to overcome obstacles, learn from failures, and persevere in the face of challenges. Ultimately, these life skills are essential for success in school, work, and relationships, and can have a lifelong impact on teens' personal and professional development.

In addition to fostering a supportive environment and developing essential life skills, it is important to encourage teens to explore their interests and passions. This can help them discover their strengths, develop new talents, and build a sense of purpose and fulfillment. By providing teens with opportunities to pursue their passions, whether through extracurricular activities, internships, volunteer work, or creative projects, we can help them develop a strong sense of identity and self-worth. This can empower them to take ownership of their futures, set ambitious goals, and pursue their dreams with determination and enthusiasm.

Furthermore, empowering teens for success also involves providing them with access to education and resources that can help them achieve their goals. This includes promoting academic excellence, providing career guidance and counseling, and connecting teens with opportunities for further education and training. By equipping teens with the knowledge, skills, and resources they need to succeed academically and professionally, we can empower them to pursue their passions, build successful careers, and make positive contributions to society. Additionally, it is important to promote lifelong learning and personal growth, encouraging teens to continue to explore new interests, expand their horizons, and adapt to an ever-changing world. By providing them with a supportive environment, essential life skills, opportunities to explore their interests, and access to education and resources, we can help teens develop the confidence, resilience, and determination they need to achieve their goals and reach their full potential. Ultimately, empowering teens for success is not just about preparing them for the challenges of today, but also equipping them with the tools and resources they need to thrive in an increasingly complex and interconnected world. By investing in the empowerment of teens, we are investing in the future of our communities and our society as a whole.

www.ingramcontent.com/pod-product-compliance
Lightning Source LLC
Chambersburg PA
CBHW070223180726
47999CB00017B/1953